Praise for *bell hooks' Spiritual Vision*

During the last days of her life, bell hooks was most concerned with the peace she found between meditation and prayer. She spoke with conviction about the importance of faith. Nadra Nittle's *bell hooks' Spiritual Vision* is important in that it highlights one of the most overlooked aspects of her personal politics—the spiritual foundation of her feminist and Baptist-informed Buddhist practice. Nittle provides the insight we need to honor hooks' holistic approach to her theoretical interventions.

—**Lynnée Denise,** friend and confidant of bell hooks

Nadra Nittle draws the reader in with an invitation to an intimate engagement, more like a conversation, with bell hooks the person, the author, and with the depth and nuances of her spirituality. Nittle offers an impeccable narrative of the profound figure and voice that is bell hooks that compels the reader to engage hooks beyond intellectual analysis but with their whole body, mind, and emotions. There is a hopefulness that Nittle brings out that can be gleaned from hooks' writing and the spiritual philosophy that guided her life. As Nittle traces the lineage to hooks' spirituality to both the pain and affirmations from her youth, I felt myself at times lamenting, while feeling empowered by hooks' honest cultural criticism and inspired by her unapologetic aspirations for a love ethic rooted in spirituality as a social force.

—**Phil Allen Jr.,** author of *Open Wounds: A Story of Racial Tragedy, Trauma, and Redemption* and *The Prophetic Lens: The Camera and Black Moral Agency from MLK to Darnella Frazier*

Nadra Nittle's *bell hooks' Spiritual Vision: Buddhist, Christian, and Feminist* is a thoughtful, intentional, and sensitive work that uplifts bell hooks as a theologian. Nittle, in her succinct reporting style, mixed with her own journey of meeting the late hooks once, grounds readers in how prolific a writer hooks was on everything from feminism to love and men—and how all of this writing was grounded in the spiritual. Nittle takes seriously, like other Black writers she cites throughout, bell hooks the theologian. Whether you are engaging with hooks for the first or tenth time, *bell hooks' Spiritual Vision: Buddhist, Christian, and Feminist* is a must-read.

—**Olga Marina Segura**, author of *Birth of a Movement: Black Lives Matter and the Catholic Church*

A sweeping overview of the cultural, political, and religious forces at work prior to and during bell hooks' lifetime, Nittle's book situates hooks' development of a syncretic and hybridized spirituality in concert with her growth into one of the preeminent feminist theorists and writers of our era. Nittle argues that hooks married spirituality and feminism successfully, creating a healing place for herself and blazing trails for the rest of us to follow. Nittle puts hooks' detractors and hooks' writing in conversation, pointing out how her opponents failed to account for the entirety and complexity of her work. It is, at times, delicious. From Beyoncé to Emma Watson, Spike Lee to Thích Nhất Hạnh, this book examines the range of hooks' influence and reach. No one is immune from her consideration, and Nittle argues that everything hooks did and wrote was animated by a fierce commitment to love as action and spirituality as liberation. Refusing to simplify or flatten out hooks' complex body of work, Nittle does justice to the beauty and power of hooks' hard-won belief systems and urges us to engage with hooks' writing in a world increasingly riven by ideological extremism and purposeful misrepresentations of feminist spiritualities. Dialectical, oppositional, accessible, insightful, informative, fascinating, nimble, incisive, and heartening, Nittle's book is both homage and love song.

—**Beth Feagan**, MFA, assistant professor, general studies, Berea College

This carefully researched and beautifully written look at the spiritual life of one of our finest writers and intellectuals is a complex and valuable addition to writing about the inimitable bell hooks. Nadra Nittle introduces readers to hooks in a way in which she is too rarely shown, and does so with complexity, grace, and wisdom. I'm so glad this book exists.

—**Silas House**, author of *Lark Ascending*

bell hooks' Spiritual Vision

bell hooks' Spiritual Vision

Buddhist, Christian, and Feminist

Nadra Nittle

FORTRESS PRESS
MINNEAPOLIS

BELL HOOKS' SPIRITUAL VISION
Buddhist, Christian, and Feminist

Library of Congress Control Number: 2023020030 (print)

Cover image: Author and cultural critic bell hooks poses for a portrait on
December 16, 1996, in New York City, New York. Photo by Karjean Levine/
Getty Images
Cover design: L. Whitt

Print ISBN: 978-1-5064-8836-3
eBook ISBN: 978-1-5064-8837-0

Contents

1. The Buddhist-Christian Love Ethic of bell hooks   1

2. The Girl with Too Much Spirit   23

3. Christianity for the Outcast   41

4. A Feminist Approach to Spirituality   55

5. Faith without Capitalism and Fundamentalism   71

6. "Love Is Everything"   87

7. New Visions of Romance and Relationships   105

Afterword   121

Notes   129

Index   143

CHAPTER ONE

The Buddhist-Christian
Love Ethic of bell hooks

I met bell hooks for the first and only time as a teenager in the 1990s. Too unfamiliar with her work to have a substantive conversation about her efforts to make feminism more race and class conscious, I sat next to her mostly in silence and awe. She'd given a speech in my school auditorium, and I was part of a group of students chosen to dine with her afterward.

A feminist theorist, cultural critic, scholar, and writer, hooks defined feminism in simple terms—as a "movement to end sexism, sexist exploitation, and oppression."[1] She also pushed for feminism to recognize the lasting impact of enslavement on Black American women. In her groundbreaking 1981 book *Ain't I a Woman: Black Women and Feminism*, hooks writes, "A devaluation of black womanhood occurred as a result of the sexual exploitation of black women during slavery that has not altered in the course of hundreds of years."[2]

When I met hooks, I had yet to read that work or any others she'd written. But I did have enough sense to bring a copy of her latest book at the time, 1995's *Killing Rage: Ending Racism*, to the meet-and-greet. She signed her name on the title page in the all-lowercase style that became her trademark. Her decision not to capitalize it derived from hooks' desire to direct attention to her work rather than herself.[3] For the same reason, hooks did not author books under her birth name, Gloria Jean Watkins. Instead, she used a nom de plume that honored her maternal great-grandmother, Bell Blair Hooks, "known for her snappy and bold tongue."[4] In my copy of *Killing Rage*, she wrote her pseudonym with flair, the stems of the letters elongated in elegant but exaggerated lines.

Since I met hooks, I have lived in more than fifteen residences, three states, and briefly in another country. There, I pulled one hooks book after another off the shelves of my university library to abate the culture shock and loneliness I experienced during my first weeks as an exchange student. It felt comforting to read the words of a Black American feminist when I was the rare Black American woman in my orbit. Today, I still have my signed hardcover copy of *Killing Rage*.

Featuring a monotype by artist Emma Amos of an American flag with an *X* on the stripes and a group of Jim Crow–era Black children in place of the stars, the jacket cover is now smudged and frayed due to the book's many moves. Although I've been careful not to lose *Killing Rage*, I haven't consulted the book often over the years. Upon learning that hooks died of renal failure at the premature age of sixty-nine on December 15, 2021, I immediately sought it out.

I was unaware that she had been ill, and the news stung. I recalled my brief meeting with her, wishing I had been sufficiently acquainted with her work then to say and ask more, and that the encounter had been more recent, so I could remember more. While I don't recall much of the speech she gave to the student body on the day we met, snippets of her lecture are embedded in my memory. At the core of her address to the school, and her interactions with students afterward, was love—a subject she devoted a chapter to in *Killing Rage* and dedicated entire books to later. It was not widely known then that hooks championed love as a remedy to the world's social problems due to a spiritual practice steeped in Buddhism and Christianity. hooks would discuss her faith in depth in the years to come, revealing the crucial role spirituality played in her politics and in her personal and professional life.

Like so many influential Black women born before her, including Toni Morrison and Mary McLeod Bethune, both of whom hooks admired, a unique spiritual vision inspired her to foster social change. hooks believed that love could defeat the intersecting forms of oppression that targeted women, children, people of color, the poor, and the otherwise marginalized. In doing so, she echoed the beliefs of one of her spiritual heroes, the Rev. Martin Luther King Jr., who wrote, "Love is the greatest force in the universe. It is the heartbeat of the moral cosmos. He who loves is a participant in the being of God."[5]

Long credited for her contributions to political thought, hooks' contributions to spiritual thought have been underrecognized even though her diverse body of work includes a love ethic informed by faith and activism. This book reframes the work of hooks to better reflect her identity as both a radical feminist and a believer—motivated by love as a force for revolution.

When hooks discussed love, she was not referring to a sentimental definition of the term. In fact, it disturbed her that so many people conflated love with the passion and infatuation one feels at the start of a courtship. In search of love's true meaning, hooks found a favorite in the definition that psychoanalyst M. Scott Peck provides in his bestselling 1978 self-help book, *The Road Less Traveled*. Also heavily influenced by Buddhism and Christianity, Peck describes love as "the will to extend one's self for the purpose of nurturing one's own or another's spiritual growth."[6] Moreover, he states, "love is as love does. Love is an act of will—namely, both an intention and an action. Will also implies choice. We do not have to love. We choose to love."[7]

hooks agreed that love is an action and viewed her writing, teaching, and speaking as loving acts. When she visited my school, hooks showed love for a type of family subjected to widespread hatred during the 1990s: low-income single women and their children. She challenged problematic narratives circulating in the media about these families, specifically the conventional wisdom that a man was all they needed to thrive. Mind you, welfare reform was a top political issue in the 1990s. Single mothers, particularly low-income single Black mothers, were vilified as "welfare queens," stemming from sensationalistic press reports and Ronald Reagan's use of this stereotype while campaigning for president years earlier.[8]

Initially, the media reports on so-called welfare queens focused on a mixed-race Chicago woman named Linda Taylor, who was convicted of welfare fraud in 1974.[9] She had also been accused of other crimes, including kidnapping and murder, but politicians left out this information and, eventually, Taylor herself when demonizing women on welfare. Rather than discussing her as one woman linked to various crimes, politicians used Taylor to suggest that all women on welfare were immoral, irresponsible, and, thus, undeserving of help.

Politicians also exploited the welfare queen trope to attack households headed by Black women, and to blame them for the social ills—juvenile delinquency, truancy, teen pregnancy, gang violence, the crack epidemic—that became talking points on both sides of the partisan aisle. In 1996, then First Lady Hillary Clinton said while discussing her husband's 1994 crime bill, "But we also have to have an organized effort against gangs. . . . We need to take these people on. They are often connected to big drug cartels; they are not just gangs of kids anymore. They are often the kinds of kids that are called superpredators—no conscience, no empathy. We can talk about why they ended up that way, but first, we have to bring them to heel."[10]

These remarks would come back to bite Clinton during her failed 2016 presidential campaign, when both Black Lives Matter activists and Republicans dug up these comments to criticize her record on racial justice. Clinton apologized for calling children superpredators, arguing that she regretted using the term and no longer felt comfortable with that characterization of troubled young people.

In the 1990s, Clinton may not have been interested in discussing how such youth "ended up that way," but both liberal and conservative pundits of the time were; they cited absent Black fathers as the major factor. This thinking was not new. It echoed the conclusion politician and sociologist Daniel Patrick Moynihan made in his 1965 report on "The Negro Family," which drew on the 1930s work of Black sociologist E. Franklin Frazier. hooks, though, questioned the idea that the simple presence of a man in a household would heal families.

During her talk at my school, hooks did not discount the important role that fathers play but emphasized that just any man in a home would not do. The presence of abusive and neglectful men in a household would in no way benefit families, she said. She brought up her own father during this discussion, pointing out that he had never loved her and that her mother validated her perceptions after years of denials. In several books, including her 1996 memoir, *Bone Black: Memories of Girlhood*, and during speaking appearances well into the last decade of her life, hooks would revisit her fractured relationship with her father.

Hearing hooks say that her father didn't love her was shocking—unsettling, even—but I found her openness about the matter incredibly brave. It is taken for granted in society that all parents love their children—unconditionally so—and taboo to state otherwise except in the most egregious cases of abuse. hooks, however, was unafraid to challenge this taboo by publicly acknowledging that her experience with an unloving parent was hardly an anomaly. Loving parents, she stressed, were what families needed.

The welfare queen myth originates from the social structure that hooks described then as "white supremacist capitalist patriarchy." Later, she would modify the phrase to "imperialist white supremacist capitalist patriarchy." The messaging about welfare recipients targeted women of color by using the crimes of one mixed-race woman—who reportedly appeared to be Black, Latina, Filipina, and even white, depending on how she styled herself—to brand all Black women reliant on the social safety net as corrupt.[11] It blamed single Black mothers for the nation's economic and social woes, ignoring that the vast majority of federal funds go toward the nation's defense budget and a fraction of that is spent on social service programs like welfare. It promoted patriarchy by emphasizing the need for men in the home and not the role systemic discrimination played in devastating Black communities and keeping Black women specifically at the bottom of the social hierarchy.

hooks, then, was not interested in whether men were in or out of the home but in dismantling imperialist white supremacist capitalist patriarchy. During a 2015 interview, hooks explained why she began to use that phrase in her work:

> We can't begin to understand the nature of domination if we don't understand how these systems connect with one another. Significantly, this phrase has always moved me because it doesn't value one system over another. For so many years in the feminist movement, women were saying that gender is the only aspect of identity that really matters, that domination only came into the world because of rape. Then we had so many race-oriented folks who were saying, "Race is the most important thing. We don't even need to be talking about class or gender." So for me, that phrase always reminds me of a global context, of the context of class, of empire, of capitalism, of racism and of patriarchy. Those things are all linked—an interlocking system.[12]

hooks believed that love was the one force that could put an end to this system of domination, for it is the source of true connection with others, she said, underscoring how important it is to lead one's life as "a sacrament of love."[13] Given hooks' philosophy, the presence of a father, or a mother, in the home did not matter as much as having love in the home to heal broken families and a broken world.

RECOGNIZING HOOKS AS A WOMAN OF FAITH

As a self-described "Buddhist Christian,"[14] hooks believed in the transformative power of love. But it took time for her to own this identity. As a young woman in the 1970s, she witnessed the leaders of the political movements she was involved in shun love and spirituality in favor of power. "I had felt pulled in all directions by anti-racist struggle, by the feminist movement, sexual liberation, by the fundamentalist Christianity of my upbringing," hooks recalled. "I wanted to embrace radical politics and still know god. I wanted to resist and be redeemed."[15]

Through the teachings of Vietnamese Buddhist monk Thích Nhất Hạnh and King, hooks found a space where there was no divide between her spiritual practice and political activism. She was baptized as a Christian in childhood and began following Buddhism as a Stanford University student after meeting some Buddhist nuns through the beat poet Gary Snyder. In the tradition of both spiritual modalities, she built her work "on a foundation of loving-kindness."[16] But she was quick to note "that you must have courage to love, that you have to have a profound will to do what is right to love, that it does not come easy," paraphrasing King's words from his 1963 sermon collection *Strength to Love*.[17]

In 1966, King and Hạnh met for the first time.[18] Both dedicated to the causes of peace and nonviolence, the spiritual leaders were not merely influences on hooks but influences on each other. They met after Hạnh wrote to King to ask him to support ending the Vietnam War, a stance King's advisors cautioned him not to take. They feared it would be a distraction from the civil rights movement and lead to a backlash against King.

During their meeting, King and Hạnh discussed peace, freedom, and community, agreeing that community is vital for progress. Afterward, King called for an end to the Vietnam War. He reasoned that speaking out against the war was in his purview as an advocate for peace. King was so impressed with Hạnh that he nominated the monk for a Nobel Peace Prize on January 25, 1967, but no Peace Prize was handed out that year.[19]

In May 1967, Hạnh and King reunited at the World Council of Churches' *Pacem in Terris* (Peace on Earth) conference in Geneva, Switzerland. At this meeting, according to the Thích Nhất Hạnh Foundation, Hạnh told King that the Vietnamese considered the civil rights activist to be a bodhisattva, or "an enlightened being trying to awaken other living beings and help them go in the direction of compassion and understanding."[20] It was their last meeting. The next year, King was assassinated in Memphis. A statue of the two men at the Magnolia Grove Monastery in Batesville, Mississippi, commemorates their exchanges and the beloved community they imagined.

Hạnh recalled later that, in loving King, he also experienced loving Jesus Christ, as King's "deep embodied love for Jesus penetrated

[Hạnh] through this energy of love."[21] The connection between these two spiritual leaders points to the connections between Buddhism and Christianity, which Hạnh explored in books such as 1995's *Living Buddha, Living Christ* and 1999's *Going Home: Jesus and Buddha as Brothers*. Hạnh died on January 22, 2022, at age ninety-five.

Characterized as a religion, a philosophy, and a spiritual practice, Buddhism first spread in India and then throughout the rest of Asia before going global. *Tricycle*, the Buddhist Review, describes Buddhism as follows:

> [It is] based on the teachings of the Buddha, or the "Awakened One,"— the title given to the Indian spiritual seeker Siddhartha Gautama after he attained enlightenment more than 2,600 years ago. The Buddha's best-known teachings, the four noble truths and the eightfold path, describe the nature of human suffering and a way to liberate oneself from the existential pain of living and achieve nirvana. . . . While the broader Buddhist family includes many different schools with their own beliefs and practices, these various traditions share a conviction that one can come to understand the truth of existence by living an ethical life dedicated to spiritual development.[22]

Christianity, in comparison, is an Abrahamic religion that began in the first century in what is now known as the Middle East and is based on the teachings of Jesus of Nazareth. Regarded by Christians as the Son of God, Jesus preached, performed miracles, and died on the cross, only to be resurrected for humanity's salvation. Although Christianity is a monotheistic religion and Buddhism is a nontheistic one, they both focus on compassion, personal transformation, action, and a call for followers to distance themselves from materialism and worldliness.

These aspects of Christianity and Buddhism deeply appealed to hooks, who said she strove to lead her life by such principles. But after she died, the role of spirituality in her life and scholarship was muted in the mainstream press. hooks was identified as a public intellectual and author of more than three dozen books spanning genres including memoir, feminist theory, cultural criticism, poetry, and children's literature, but the fact that she identified as a woman of faith was mentioned in passing or not at all in her obituaries. The oversight was glaring, given that in the few decades preceding her death, hooks made a point to share her spiritual philosophy in detail with the world.

She may not have been an official minister, but hooks used her writing, teaching, and public appearances to engage in what amounted to preaching. She urged her readers to contemplate how they could be more loving and how society would be more loving without a system of domination based on race, class, gender, and empire. In using her work to preach, hooks followed in the tradition of the many Black women before her who did not let the fact that they were unordained hinder them from instructing their communities on the importance of faith, hope, and love.

But hooks did have concerns about being an uncredentialed woman who dared to lead spiritual discourse. In an essay, she recalled her fears ahead of her talk at a conference on Buddhism and women. While other speakers were scheduled to present their lectures in a chapel, hooks was slated to give hers in a secular space she described as "a cavernous auditorium."[23] She worried that the conference organizers were making a judgment about her spiritual authenticity by arranging for her talk to occur someplace decidedly not a sanctuary. In the end, hooks felt a sacred presence in the auditorium and a "loving-kindness"attached to her words as she gave her speech.[24] But before the event, she worried:

> I was not seen as a "real" Buddhist—no long time with a teacher, no journey to India or Tibet, never present at important retreats—definitely someone engaged in buddhadharma [Buddha's teachings] without credentials. The two companions who had joined me at the conference listened with compassion to my whining. "Why did I have to speak in a huge auditorium? Why did I have to speak on a Friday night?" "Yes," I told them, "lots of people might want to hear bell hooks speak on feminist theory and cultural criticism, but that's not the same as a talk about Buddhism."[25]

The works of Toni Morrison depict how unordained Black women have a tradition of inviting the sacred into spaces that aren't official sanctuaries, be it in their homes or places in nature. In Morrison's debut novel, 1970's *The Bluest Eye*, a healer named M'Dear can go into ailing people's homes and facilitate the healing that the town preacher and Scripture alone cannot. In *Beloved*, Baby Suggs leads worship services in the woods, teaching the Black community how to love themselves after their exploitation and brutalization while enslaved.

hooks appreciated Morrison, writing her 1983 PhD dissertation at the University of California, Santa Cruz, on the novelist's literature.[26] Morrison's success as a writer helped hooks envision herself as one, but hooks also enjoyed Morrison's fiction because it centered the Black women and girls relegated to the margins of literature historically. About an abused Black girl who longs for blue eyes, *The Bluest Eye* was one of hooks' favorite novels. hooks would depart from her writing on feminist theory and cultural criticism to write children's books such as 1999's *Happy to Be Nappy* to foster a love of Blackness in youth of color before white supremacy instilled in them internalized racism and poor self-image.

"The bell hooks work that really matters to me are the children's books because I feel like I wrote those books with much greater political intent in the sense of wanting to say, 'How do we begin to free the Black girl body, the Black boy body, before they have undergone years and years of emotional assault and colonization?'" hooks asked in 2014.[27]

The most significant trait that hooks and Morrison shared is their interest in writing to help others. Morrison wanted her troubled characters to experience a journey that would put them on the path of resilience, learning valuable lessons along the way that could inspire readers. hooks had a similar mission. "I want my work to be about healing," she said during a 2018 interview. "I am a fortunate writer because every day of my life, practically, I get a letter, a phone call, from someone who tells me how my work has transformed their life."[28]

hooks was a woman of faith, a believer in the transformative power of love, and such outcomes were her ultimate objective. The mainstream media may have ignored the importance of spirituality in hooks' work, but religious publications did not. The *National*

Catholic Reporter, for example, published a feature article months after hooks' death about what her writing and teaching meant to Black Catholics. Theologian LaRyssa D. Herrington, the article's author, wrote that hooks believed that a commitment to spiritual practice required conscious effort and a willingness to match one's thoughts with one's actions. Herrington states,

> The legacy of bell hooks' life is that genuine faith gives birth to works: works of advocacy, of dismantling systems of power, of undoing internalized self-hatred, and eliminating hierarchies that seek to kill, divide and destroy. hooks understood action, along with love, as a sacrament— "[a] visible form of an invisible spirit, an outward manifestation of an inward power." She believed that spirituality and the spiritual life were the centers out of which we gather the strength to love and in turn, empower one to protest and resist.[29]

hooks writes in her 2000 book *All About Love: New Visions* that, for years, many of her friends and colleagues did not know that she "was devoted to a spiritual practice."[30] In the academy, it was more acceptable to embrace atheism than to be passionately devoted to a "divine spirit," so she did not broadcast her beliefs.[31] hooks also worried that others would think she was proselytizing if she discussed her faith, but, eventually, she felt it was important to share the benefits of her spiritual practice. She wanted people to understand how she could still have hope while living in an imperialist white supremacist capitalist patriarchy.

In *All About Love*, she states that she began to be more transparent about the place of spirituality in her life to comfort her students struggling with hopelessness, loneliness, and lovelessness. "When young, bright, beautiful students would come to my office and confess their despondency, I felt it was irresponsible to just listen and commiserate with their woes without daring to show how I had confronted similar issues in my life," she writes. "Often, they would urge me to tell them how I sustained my joy in living. To tell the truth, I had to be willing to talk openly about spiritual life."[32]

Six years before her death, hooks revealed in an interview that her spiritual practice from both Buddhism and Christianity was the foundation for her life. They grounded her, taught her discipline and the ability to self-interrogate, she said. She may have been a writer and a feminist, but the ethical-spiritual values she stood on as an adult came from Christianity and Buddhism. Feminism did not ground her and writing did not teach her discipline, but her spiritual practice did. "I've been coming out more and more in the fact that the work that I'm writing is about spirituality," she said.[33]

Some titles of her works—*Remembered Rapture*, *Salvation*, *Communion*, and *Rock My Soul*—make obvious their spiritual focus. Others, such as *All About Love*, require one to read the book to learn that hooks prayed regularly and enjoyed reading how the Bible describes love in Song of Solomon and 1 Corinthians. The book also highlights many of her spiritual influences. In addition to Hạnh, King, and Peck, they include American Trappist monk Thomas Merton, Vietnamese Buddhist nun Sister Chân Không, and Spanish Carmelite nun Teresa of Ávila.

Through her work, hooks chose to love, instruct, challenge, and share, especially about her political and spiritual journeys. Upon her death, she was the distinguished professor in residence at Berea College in her native Kentucky. Berea is home of the bell hooks center, one of many great honors hooks earned, including the American Book Award. The institution has an abolitionist history, tuition-free admission, and a Christian identity based on a gospel of "impartial love."[34]

Although Christianity's message about love resonated with hooks, and she argued that the church once served as "the primary system that ever promoted healing in Black people,"[35] the radical feminist also questioned patriarchy and capitalism in the church. She acknowledged that the church nurtured her as a child and as an adult, but she was not afraid to call out its role in sexism, classism, and other systems of oppression. She adopted a similar mindset about Buddhism. Inspired by Hạnh's socially engaged approach to the faith, hooks found his writing on women to be rooted "in the traditional role of nurturer, and separate from the world of warriorship and lineage that is so clearly defined as male."[36]

For hooks, love did not mean keeping quiet. She called out in love, a practice for which she drew public ire at times. "When I write provocative social and cultural criticism that causes readers to stretch their minds, to think beyond set paradigms, I think of that work as love in action," she said. "While it may challenge, disturb and at times even frighten or enrage readers, love is always the place where I begin and end."[37]

THE BACKLASH AGAINST BELL HOOKS

As a radical feminist critic, hooks faced a sustained public backlash for raising concerns about the image and impact of one of the world's most beloved recording artists—Beyoncé.

In 2014, hooks took part in a panel discussion called "Are You Still a Slave? Liberating the Black Female Body" at The New School's Eugene Lang College of Liberal Arts, where she was then a scholar-in-residence.[38] During the conversation, she revealed that the cover image of Beyoncé on *Time*'s 100 Most Influential People issue alarmed her, as the singer has vacant eyes, parted lips, and a see-through top. Underneath the top, she wears garments that have been described as either two-piece underwear or swimwear.

"Isn't this interesting that she's being supposedly held up as one of the most important people in our nation, in the world, and, yet, why did they image her [like this]?" hooks asked. "What is that cover meant to say about the Black female body?" Eventually, hooks answered her own questions. With the cover, she said, the editorial team had decided, "Let's take the image of this super rich, very powerful Black female, and let's use it in the service of imperialist white supremacist capitalist patriarchy."[39]

hooks explained that she consistently made connections between the hypersexualized, enslaved Black female body and the predatory lens through which bodies of all women are framed today. Given this context, *Time*'s cover of Beyoncé was not "a liberatory image," she said.[40] Liberatory images, according to hooks, portray independence and power and counter hegemony by not conceding to established conventions of how women should appear.

hooks didn't just object to the *Time* cover because of Beyoncé's exposed undergarments. She also disliked it because the singer looks like a "deer in headlights" on the cover. The magazine took one of the world's most influential Black women and defanged her by stripping her body of clothing and her countenance of character. With a blank stare and a half-nude body in a society where naked bodies have historically conveyed powerlessness, nowhere more so than the auction block, Beyoncé is devoid of agency on the *Time* cover.

When told that the singer likely approved the cover shot and the wardrobe, hooks was not swayed. "You're saying, then, that from my deconstructive point of view that she's colluding in the construction of herself as a slave?" she asked. Shortly afterward, hooks added the remarks that sparked continued public outrage against her. "I see a part of Beyoncé that is, in fact, anti-feminist, that is assaulting, that is a terrorist, in the sense of . . . the impact on young girls. . . . I actually feel like the major assault on feminism in our society has come from visual media and from television and videos."[41]

When hooks said "terrorist," she was referring to how imagery linked to Beyoncé the corporate entity does not create a new standard for women but leans into imperialist white supremacist capitalist patriarchy. On the *Time* cover, hooks argued that the anesthetized look on the singer's face and her plain white underwear make her appear childlike—more prey than powerful woman—which sends a harmful message to young girls. "One could argue, even more than her body, it's what that body stands for, the body of desire fulfilled— that is wealth, fame, celebrity, all the things that so many people in our culture are lusting for, wanting," hooks said.[42]

As for hooks suggesting that "a part of Beyoncé . . . is a terrorist," it's worth noting that she used this provocative term frequently to describe a wide range of behaviors and situations. In *All About Love*, the term appears multiple times; she calls the womanizing men that others might simply label "players" or lotharios "intimate terrorists," for example.[43] But hooks could've made all the same points about

Beyoncé's *Time* cover without using the term. By invoking it to be provocative, she likely turned off members of the public who might have otherwise been open to her thoughts on the problematic framing of Black women in media. At the same time, she might have very well chosen the term *terrorist* because she felt that Black women have been terrorized by historic constructions of themselves as oversexed and, thus, "unrapeable," making them vulnerable to sexual exploitation in the past and present.

While hooks did not mention her spiritual practice when discussing the *Time* magazine cover, it almost certainly factored into the concerns she raised about the characterization of Black women as hypersexual. In her 2006 book *Homegrown: Engaged Cultural Criticism*, she expresses dismay that more "African Americans have not been interested in reclaiming representations of Black Madonnas."[44] Although images of the Virgin Mary with pale skin have been normalized, paintings of her with dark skin date back to antiquity and can be found all over the world—from Cartagena, Colombia, to Częstochowa, Poland. hooks posited that images of the Dark Virgin could inspire Black Americans just as they have for other groups such as Indigenous Mexicans and Afro-descendants throughout the Americas. She wondered what needed to happen in the United States to reframe "the Black female not as whore, bitch, bearer of violence," she states, "but as bearer of the sacred, the healing, the inspiring."[45]

Ironically, in the years after hooks objected to the *Time* cover of Beyoncé, the singer appropriated imagery of the Virgin Mary and West African goddesses in music videos, musical performances, and even the pregnancy and birth announcements of her twins, Rumi and Sir. But hooks likely would've taken issue with some of this imagery, such as Beyoncé's 2016 pregnancy announcement via Instagram in a veil, bra, and panties. Just months before the pregnancy, Beyoncé released her visual album *Lemonade*, which hooks critiqued in a *Guardian* piece called "Beyoncé's Lemonade Is Capitalist Money-Making at Its Best." In the review, hooks' feminism and nonviolence as a Buddhist Christian join together to challenge the messaging of the visual album starring a fictionalized Beyoncé as a wronged woman.

After a lover's betrayal in the "Hold Up" video, Beyoncé takes to the streets with a baseball bat, smashing cars while wearing a mustard-colored Roberto Cavalli gown, which hooks describes as "sexy" in her review.[46] B. Akerlund, the "Hold Up" video's costume designer and stylist, did as well. "It was flowing . . . it was see-through . . . it had all these different shapes and was still sexy," Akerlund said in an interview about *Lemonade*. "With the context of the video being a little bit violent, we were really looking for something of the opposite to make it flirty and positive and sexy and to sort of enhance a woman's strengths."[47]

Akerlund's description of the couture gown and its message is exactly what hooks objected to about *Lemonade*. hooks asserts in her review that the visual album intends to "seduce" while promoting violence. She states,

> Contrary to misguided notions of gender equality, women do not and will not seize power and create self-love and self-esteem through violent acts. Female violence is no more liberatory than male violence. And when violence is made to look sexy and eroticized, as in the Lemonade sexy dress street scene, it does not serve to undercut the prevailing cultural sentiment that it is acceptable to use violence to reinforce domination, especially in relations between men and women. Violence does not create positive change.[48]

hooks struggled to control her own rage in the aftermath of failed romantic relationships. When she first met Thích Nhất Hạnh, she confessed that she was ashamed of how much anger she still harbored toward a partner. Hạnh told her to compost the anger, to transform it into useful energy—"understanding and compassion."[49] As a practitioner of nonviolence informed by Buddhist and Christian principles, hooks condemned the glamorized violence in "Hold Up," but her feminism contributed to this decision as well. She believed that feminism was about more than equal rights for men and women and that dismantling patriarchy required the eradication of violence and domination. "Patriarchy has no gender,"[50] according to hooks, meaning that women and men alike can perpetuate it through physical, emotional, and other forms of intimidation. In the *Lemonade* visual album, Beyoncé exhibits domination by smashing car windows, a violent act that will result in no meaningful resolution or reconnection between her and her partner.

"I think it serves the interest of domination if the only way people can respond to victimage is rage," hooks said during a 1992 interview. "Because then they really are just mirroring the very conditions that brought them into victimization. Violence. The conquering of other people's territory."[51]

Beyoncé's real-life husband, hip-hop mogul Jay-Z, makes an appearance in the visual album before *Lemonade* ends. hooks, however, is not sure the tender images of him can be trusted because he is not shown doing any work to heal himself and his relationship. "No matter how hard women in relationships with patriarchal men work for change, forgive and reconcile, men must do the work of inner and outer transformation if emotional violence against black females is to end," hooks writes. "We see no hint of this in Lemonade."[52]

Although hooks offers plenty of criticism about *Lemonade*, she notes that it stands out by displaying Black women of various ages, body types, and social classes, albeit in a fantasy setting with couture fashion and high-end sportswear, a market Beyoncé entered in 2016 with her Ivy Park clothing line. The visual album features the mothers of the slain Black boys and men who kickstarted the Black Lives Matter Movement. It honors Black elders and ancestors and gives voice to the pain of Black women who have been dehumanized and devalued historically. "It challenges us all to look anew, to radically revision how we see the black female body," hooks states.[53]

But *Lemonade* could've gone deeper, she continues. Rather than equating Black womanhood with victimhood, hooks wished the visual album would've shown Black women on the path to self-actualization. Here, hooks' Buddhism was at play. In that philosophy, there are no limits to what individuals can actualize if they lose the construct of self. hooks chose her great-grandmother's name as a pseudonym, in part, to distance herself from Gloria Jean Watkins, her birth name and the self to which she clung most. The decision was "not dissimilar really to the new names that accompany all ordinations in Muslim, Buddhist, Catholic traditions," she said in 1992. "Everyone in my life calls me Gloria. When I do things that involve work, they will often speak of me as 'bell,' but part of it has been a practice of not being attached to either of those."[54]

In Zen Buddhism, Taoism, and humanistic psychology, the self-actualized person—the one who has lost attachment to self—has "caring and responsible interpersonal relationships"[55] and not the volatile relationships depicted in *Lemonade*. Rather than focusing on violence, pain, and glamor, *Lemonade* could have portrayed spiritual and emotional healing, hooks argues. Since it did not, Beyoncé's "construction of feminism cannot be trusted," she writes. "Her vision of feminism does not call for an end to patriarchal domination."[56]

For writing a nuanced but clearly critical review of *Lemonade*, hooks drew the ire of not only Beyoncé fans but millennial and Gen X Black feminists who teamed up for a written roundtable in the singer's defense. Although hooks' review did not attack Beyoncé on a personal level, some of the attacks against hooks were personal. Having already been characterized as old and out of touch for objecting to the *Time* cover,[57] she was accused of embracing respectability politics and anti-Blackness after her *Lemonade* critique. The response was stunning, given that most reviews of *Lemonade* had been positive and that hooks' one critical review would do little to stop the album's momentum. In her 1992 book, *Black Looks: Race and Representation*, hooks writes about Madonna, describing the challenges of critiquing an iconic entertainer. Her insights then are just as applicable to the Beyoncé controversy.

> Sometimes it is difficult to find words to make a critique when we find ourselves attracted by some aspect of a performer's act and disturbed by others, or when a performer shows more interest in promoting progressive social causes than is customary, we may see that performer as above critique. Or we may feel our critique will in no way intervene in the worship of them as a cultural icon.[58]

What's more is that some of hooks' loudest detractors showed little familiarity with her work, particularly her stances against violence, patriarchy, and capitalism, which she has invoked repeatedly in her pop culture reviews. She didn't even go easy on a family film such as 1990's *Home Alone*, which she questioned for "celebrat[ing] disobedience and violence."[59] Three years later, she criticized Spike Lee's *Malcolm X* for portraying both Black and white women as "either virgins or whores, madonnas or prostitutes."[60] She also objected to Lee leaving out influential women in Malcolm X's life, making him decidedly unmilitant, and commodifying his image. Just as she said that *Lemonade* sought to "seduce" viewers, she wrote that "Malcolm X seduce[s] us to forget the brutal realities that created black militancy."[61]

hooks knew then that criticizing the works of Black creators comes with risks. "Black critics of the movie risk being seen as traitors to the race, or as personally hostile to Spike," she writes in her review of *Malcolm X* for *Artforum*.[62] This is exactly what happened when she analyzed Beyoncé's *Lemonade* album and *Time* magazine cover, although she never made her criticism of the singer personal. Yes, she said that she sees "a part of Beyoncé that is, in fact, anti-feminist, that is assaulting, that is a terrorist," but this comment referred to the imagery associated with Beyoncé the brand and its impact on young girls. Moreover, she began her critique by holding *Time* magazine responsible for the cover and absolving Beyoncé of blame. While reviewing *Lemonade*, hooks directed her concerns to the visuals and made it clear she was referring to "the Beyoncé character,"[63] not Beyoncé the individual.

In her 1993 *Malcolm X* review, hooks agrees with filmmaker Marlon Riggs that "silencing" Black critics "prevents the development of black cultural criticism."[64] She quotes Riggs, who died the following year, discussing the unique dilemma Black reviewers face. He said,

> Even when it is clear that the critique is trying to empower and trying to heal certain wounds within our communities, there is not any space within our culture to constructively critique. There is an effort simply to shut people up in order to reify these gods, if you will, who have delivered some image of us which seems to affirm our existence in this world. As if they make up for the lack, but in fact they don't. They can become part of the hegemony.[65]

Upon *Lemonade*'s release, untold numbers of women flocked to social media to say that they felt affirmed by how it featured Black women, the poetry of Warsan Shire, and a lover's betrayal. hooks was not immune to the album's powerful reframing of Black women. "Honoring the self, loving our bodies, is an appropriate stage in the construction of healthy self-esteem," hooks writes. "This aspect of Lemonade is affirming. Certainly, to witness Miss Hattie, the 90-year-old grandmother of Jay Z, give her personal testimony that she has survived by taking the lemons life handed her and making lemonade is awesome."[66] But because hooks also criticizes the album, others tried to shut her up, as Riggs would put it.

hooks' detractors suggested that she was prudish, despite her 1997 magazine interview with the sexually explicit rapper Lil' Kim in which she remarked, "More dangerous than any words that come out of Lil' Kim's mouth are the forces of repressive puritanical morality that seek to silence her."[67] Although hooks dedicated decades of work to making feminism more inclusive of Black women's struggles, her critics insinuated that she was anti-Black for dismissing the feminism of a Black woman like Beyoncé while purportedly embracing the feminism of white *Harry Potter* star Emma Watson.[68] hooks did befriend Watson, but she also picked apart the Hermione Granger character that made the actress famous. In a 2016 interview with Watson, hooks challenged the character's feminism, pointing out how much this "girl who was just so intelligent, who is such a thinker" is "placed in the service of boy power."[69] As she continued speaking to Watson, during the very year *Lemonade* was released, she offered additional criticisms of Hermione Granger. hooks was committed to her feminist principles no matter the subject of her critiques.

But the backlash over hooks' critiques of Beyoncé's *Lemonade* album and *Time* magazine cover threaten to overshadow her contributions to feminism. When hooks died, a *Washington Post* contributor objected to the title of hooks' *Lemonade* review—"capitalist money-making at its best"—and suggested that the feminist scholar was just "as susceptible to the perils of misogyny and respectability politics as anyone else."[70] hooks never indicated that behaving in a respectable manner would end racial and gender oppression, the argument champions of respectability politics make. And her concerns about *Lemonade* did not stem from misogyny but from her desire to dismantle patriarchal norms. Her radical feminism and Buddhist-Christian ethics led her to object to the glamorized violence depicted in the visual album, which she deemed an endorsement of both patriarchy and capitalism.

hooks actually left out of her review that Beyoncé promotes capitalism in her lyrics. The singer brags in *Lemonade*'s first single, "Formation," about her designer duds—Givenchy dresses and Roc necklaces—in the tradition of male rappers like Jay-Z. Beyoncé also advises listeners, "Always stay gracious, best revenge is your paper."[71] hooks interrogated the capitalistic, patriarchal approach to power in *Lemonade* because she didn't believe it would provide Black women, or men, with spiritual and emotional liberation.

The day after her death, the *New York Times* acknowledged that "hooks' assessment [of Beyoncé] was more nuanced than the headline-making quotes suggested,"[72] but the attacks hooks faced for critiquing the singer took a toll. hooks' friend DJ Lynnée Denise, an artist, scholar, and writer, wrote a viral tweet in the months after her death condemning the "mean-spirited protection of Beyoncé and the willingness to dispose of people who challenge her." She added that this type of behavior is "why bell hooks died with a broken heart."[73]

This hardly means that hooks had lost all support when she died; the fact that Denise's tweet went viral is a testament to how many people continued to support the feminist theorist. And in the *New York Times* obituary about her life, Kimberlé Crenshaw—the law professor who coined the term *intersectionality* to describe overlapping systems of oppression—called hooks "utterly courageous in terms of putting on paper thoughts that many of us might have had in private."[74]

That courage, whether to call out Beyoncé's *Lemonade* or Spike Lee's *Malcolm X*, derived from her spiritual practice. In Hạnh and King, hooks had examples of what it looked like to pair social action with spirituality, even when it was unpopular to do so. She wed her radical feminism with her Buddhist-Christian ethic in hopes of demonstrating how a work, or even the world, could be improved with more love and less domination.

When hooks visited my school in the 1990s, she hinted that her interest in love, liberation, and domination began in her youth. Her girlhood in a hurting family in racially segregated Kentucky during the 1950s and '60s would inspire her to fight racism, classism, and sexism, and search for the true meaning of love and a spiritual practice representative of it.

"It was a tremendous liberatory moment in my painful childhood, when I thought, 'I am more than my pain,'" she recalled. "When I'm genuinely victimized by racism in my daily life, I want to be able to name it, to name that it hurts me, to say that I'm victimized by it. But I don't want to see that as all that I am."[75]

CHAPTER TWO

The Girl with Too Much Spirit

In the foreword to 1996's *Bone Black: Memories of Girlhood*, bell hooks spells out why *The Bluest Eye* became one of her favorite books. Though she was still in her teens when the novel debuted in 1970, the book did not move hooks merely because it includes Black girls. It touched her because it portrays Black girls as critical thinkers and storytellers. These young characters grapple with issues such as race, class, and identity as well as with how to address their profound emotional pain. In them, hooks saw herself during her coming of age. "My life was never going to be the same after reading this book," she states.[1]

Born September 25, 1952, Gloria Jean Watkins grew up one of seven children—six girls and one boy—in Hopkinsville, Kentucky. She had a modest upbringing with a father, Veodis Watkins, who worked as a janitor for the Postal Service, and a mother, Rosa Bell Watkins, who worked primarily as a homemaker.[2] hooks describes a tortured relationship with both parents in *Bone Black*, a memoir written in lyrical prose that highlights the fact that hooks wasn't just a theorist, essayist, and critic but also a poet. A case in point is hooks' favorite line from the book of creative nonfiction. In it, she describes spending time with her grandfather as a little girl: "When I was much smaller I sat there cuddled in his lap like a cat, hardly moving, hardly alive so near to the stillness of death was the bliss I knew in his arms."[3]

With simple language that reflects her youthful innocence, hooks' memoir doesn't follow a conventional structure, for it is not a complete retelling of her childhood but an assortment of detailed and often dreamlike memories. If there's one thread that runs throughout *Bone Black,* it's that hooks—whose girlhood name of Gloria I will use while discussing the memoir—spends her youth feeling like an outsider in her own household. Her traumatic childhood pinpoints why she would grow up to become bell hooks, a woman of faith opposed to sexism, capitalism, violence, and corporal punishment. As much as the book is a record of the abuse hooks endured as a child, *Bone Black* is equally a history of Gloria's spiritual awakening that prompts her to recognize her worth and discover where she belongs.

Audacious, intelligent, and willful, Gloria suffers in a family that doesn't know what to make of her giftedness. In addition to being a voracious reader, she dares to share her opinions during a time when many parents abided by the adage that children should be seen and not heard. Her boldness, for the time period, anyway, ends with her parents physically and emotionally violating her.

African Americans of that generation used aggressive discipline methods, in part, to compel their children to conform amid Jim Crow, the nation's system of racial apartheid that allowed white supremacists to terrorize Black people of all ages with impunity. Powerless during the era of segregation, and enslavement before then, some Black parents dehumanized their children just as a racially stratified society had dehumanized them.

In her book *Post Traumatic Slave Syndrome*, author Joy DeGruy writes that the effects of trauma are transmitted through generations, with many parents raising their children as they were raised. "Today, the African American community is made up of individuals and families who collectively share differential anxiety and adaptive survival behaviors passed down from prior generations of African Americans, many of whom likely suffered from PTSD," she argues.[4]

Today, a number of Black parents continue to use harsh forms of discipline that harken back to eras when Black children needed to quickly obey after behavioral transgressions. During segregation and enslavement, Black families feared that if they did not get their children to fall in line immediately, the children would act out in front of their white oppressors and face grave consequences.

In *Bone Black*, hooks describes the devastation of growing up with parents who crush her self-expression. Using the third person to describe herself as a child, she recalls, "She wants to express herself—to speak her mind. To them it is just talking back. Each time she opens her mouth she risks punishment. They punish her so often she feels they persecute her."[5]

As the family's scapegoat, or "problem child," as hooks puts it, Gloria is brutalized by both parents in ways that would be condemned as child abuse today. She remembers her father beating her with a wooden board and whippings with switches for routine childhood misdeeds such as arguing with a sibling and "talking back" to her mother. hooks recalls the fallout after one such incident.

> She was sent to bed without dinner. She was told to stop crying, to make no sound or she would be whipped more. No one could talk to her and she could talk to no one. She could hear him telling the mama that the girl had too much spirit, that she had to learn to mind, that that spirit had to be broken.[6]

Black American lore has long celebrated spirited men who resisted white supremacy through their will and wit. These folk heroes include Stagolee, an outlaw, and High John the Conqueror, a trickster who uses his smarts to defy his oppressors. "The victories of Stagolee and of High John the Conqueror embodied [the African American] struggle for dignity," writes the Rev. James Cone in *God of the Oppressed*.[7] But African American fables don't celebrate spirited Black women in the same way despite their long history of using cleverness and cunning to resist their white enslavers, be it poisoning food, feigning incompetence, or starting fires on plantations. In a nation that has condoned sexual and physical violence against Black women since its founding, Gloria's father wants to break her not only because he embraces patriarchal domination but also because society punishes Black women and girls who are openly spirited.

Historically one of the groups in the country with the fewest rights, Black women are not supposed to be spirited but to accept subjugation, violence, and exploitation as their lot in life. Gloria does not conduct herself as if she is inherently inferior to males, adults, and the myriad other groups society deems more valuable than little Black girls, a group that Morrison wrote about in *The Bluest Eye* because she felt they were "the most vulnerable, the most helpless unit in the society."[8]

For daring to behave in a way that transgresses the social order, Gloria faces repeated repercussions. Her family rejects her because they fear she will end up on a life path that doesn't result in a husband, children, and, presumably, economic security. They warn that her intelligence is a problem because men don't like smart women. In addition to shaming her for having a skinny body that lacks the curves men are said to prefer, they force her to eat all the food on her plate each night—even if it takes her well beyond dinnertime to do so. The punishment for noncompliance or taking too long is a beating, which Gloria often finds herself on the receiving end of when she literally can't stomach the food she's served.

Gloria's interest in classic literature is also met with suspicion, but the family is relieved when she begins devouring romance novels, a pursuit they deem more acceptable for a growing girl. Concerns about her sexuality are ever present. Her parents worry that she will turn out to be "funny," the euphemism used in her community for gay people. When her parents spot her hugging a white friend who drops her off one evening, they chastise Gloria for engaging in what they believe to be a lesbian relationship. In reality, she was comforting her classmate because the girl had attempted suicide shortly before this exchange.

Reading how often Gloria is beaten, scolded, and scapegoated is excruciating. Especially disturbing is that each family member seems to gain psychological validation from targeting her. Once her closest sibling, her brother begins making fun of her because it will boost his standing in a family that has singled her out as the problem child. On a different occasion, Gloria's father beats her for talking back to her mother, and her mother smiles in a show of approval. Later, her mother starts to routinely beat and pick on her to appease Gloria's father, for he has long disliked his gifted daughter. As an adult, hooks said that her father never once said he loved her.[9] In *Bone Black*, she writes,

> She tries to remember a time when she felt loved by him. She remembers it as being the time when she was a baby girl, a small girl. She remembers him taking her places, taking her to the world inhabited by black men, the barbershop, the pool hall. He took his affections away from her abruptly. She never understood why, only that they went and did not come back. She remembered trying to do whatever she could to bring them back, only they never came. Growing up she stopped trying. He mainly ignored her. She mainly tried to stay out of his way.[10]

The memoir does not make the source of this dislike clear, but it insinuates that there may be concerns about Gloria's paternity. Her skin color is shades lighter than that of her siblings, and she has a looser hair texture than they do, too. These physical differences make some of her relatives treat her with suspicion, even though the book offers explanations for them: her immediate ancestors have white, Black, and Native American heritage. Her light skin, then, is not hard evidence of an affair, but the family tensions related to her mother's supposed infidelities never disappear. In one of the rare scenes of violence in which Gloria is not the target, her father beats her mother bloody. While raging, he shouts at his wife, "Words about other men, about phone calls, about how he *told her*."[11]

Gloria and her siblings have no idea what their father told their mother previously. She does know that her paternal grandmother never wanted her father to marry her mother and made her mother "miserable with her lies."[12] She does not specify what these lies are but recalls that even as a small child she knew that this grandmother with coal-black skin "did not care for [her] because her face was not even thinking about being brown enough, was not even changing in the sun."[13] The "miserable lies" coupled with the questions about Gloria's complexion indicate that this is not merely an instance of skin tone bias on her grandmother's part. Rather, the grandmother is concerned that Gloria is not her son's biological child or is, at least, using Gloria's light brown skin tone to feign this concern and justify dislike of her daughter-in-law.

Growing up in a family that rejects her from the outset of her young life traumatizes Gloria. She engages in self-harm such as burning herself with an iron during one of her mother's tirades, and she internalizes her family's warning that she will "end up crazy, locked up, alone."[14] She does not try to kill herself like her white friend does, but she shows signs of acute depression—crying regularly and inconsolably. For exhibiting such symptoms, she is again ridiculed by her family.

All around her, Gloria sees "women and men . . . in distress, feeling pain, waiting for the rescue that never came," she writes. "She saw herself as one of them. She was one of those children who had come to believe that it was somehow all a mistake that she had been born into this family, into this life of never being able to do anything right, of endless torment."[15]

As an adult, hooks championed children's rights to prevent more young people from suffering as she had. Her advocacy for children would influence a socioreligious movement known as child liberation theology.

CHILD LIBERATION THEOLOGY

hooks' upbringing led her to call for a liberative approach to parenting in books such as *Feminism Is for Everybody* and *All About Love*. She supported parenting that respected the rights of children and prioritized giving them safe spaces to grow into empowered adults.

"Until we live in a culture that not only respects but also upholds basic civil rights for children, most children will not know love," hooks states in *All About Love*. "In our culture the private family dwelling is the one institutionalized sphere of power that can easily be autocratic and fascistic."[16]

She contends that abuse and love cannot coexist, and abusive parents who insist they are loving prime their children to enter abusive relationships as adults. Truly keeping children safe in homes requires ending patriarchal domination, according to hooks, who notes that both men and women oppress children through practices such as corporal punishment that involve "a more powerful person inflicting physical pain on a less powerful person in order to get a desired result."[17] Lacking the power to protest parental domination, children are the most at risk in an imperialist white supremacist capitalist patriarchy that deems them the "property" of their adult caretakers.

"I can remember vividly my mother saying to me, 'You're mine, and I'll kill you if I want to,'" hooks revealed during a 2015 discussion at Eugene Lang College. "I mean, imagine that kind of trauma on a child where this person that is really the person who cares for me the most, but she was also the person who was meanest in trying to keep me in line . . . for some system that was not a system that affirmed her or any of us."[18] hooks' family internalized the messages of subjugation and anti-Blackness imparted to them during enslavement, leading to generations of traumatized children.

Unlike women, hooks notes, children are limited in their ability to challenge their oppressors via legal means or political demonstrations. They can only hope that a caring adult can intervene for them if they suffer mistreatment in their homes. In a social hierarchy based partly on skin color, Black youth have even less influence than their white counterparts. In *Bone Black*, Gloria and her siblings have no power to stand up to a grandmother who has disparaged the Watkins children with the darkest skin.

"They want to protect each other from all forms of humiliation but cannot," she writes. "They stand cringing and weeping inside saying nothing. They do not want to be whipped with the black leather strap with holes in it hanging on the wall. They know their place. They are children. They are black. They are next to nothing."[19]

Supporters of child liberation theology have referenced hooks' argument that parenting needs to be liberative instead of domination based. Liberation theologies explore Christianity through the lens of the oppressed. It "finds Jesus on the underside of history: among those abused and cast aside by the powers-that-be," according to R. L. Stollar, theologian and children's rights advocate. He states,

> Black liberation theology declares God is Black. Mujerista theology says God is a Latina woman. Queer theology identifies God as queer. In similar fashion, child liberation theology makes clear: God is *child*, too! This is both literal and figurative. When God became human, God became a human child. God went through every stage of child development that other children do. But as child liberation theologian Janet Pais argues, Jesus is forever the *Child* of God as well, making childness an inherent part of the Trinity. Seeing God as Child means we not only understand that children are made in the image of God. It means children also bear the exact same worth and value that adults do.[20]

Proponents of child liberation theology challenge the idea that young people have no rights or that they must reach adulthood to achieve full humanity. They oppose corporal punishment and child abuse of all kinds in recognition that these acts can have detrimental effects on the emotional, mental, and spiritual development of youth. They also advocate for solutions to the food insecurity, poverty, and absent medical care that endanger children's lives worldwide.

They believe that when they receive a child in Christ's name, they receive Christ and cite Scripture to make this case. In Mark 10:14–16, Jesus scolds his disciples for preventing a group of children from approaching him. He explains that the kingdom of God belongs to young people, too. "Truly I tell you, whoever does not receive the kingdom of God as a little child will never enter it," Jesus says (v. 15 NRSV). Then "he laid his hands on them, and blessed them" (v. 16 NRSV). His actions demonstrate that the humanity of children is equal to that of adults. Although his disciples treat the little children as nuisances, Jesus shows that he understands their inherent value. His kindness to the children indicates that the "last shall be first, and the first last."[21]

When Gloria and her siblings learn the lyrics to the hymn stating "Jesus loves the little children of the world, red and yellow, black and white, they are precious in his sight," they repeat them over and over again.[22] But the veracity of the lyrics don't sway most of the adults in their lives, who continue to overlook young people's intrinsic worth. Still, Gloria is convinced that Jesus does understand and respect children, making her an early believer in child liberation theology.

Although Jesus's compassion to children has been celebrated, Scriptures have long been used to justify the oppression of children. The fourth commandment tells children to "honor your father and mother,"[23] but many Christians have ignored that parents should in turn honor their children as they would the Christ child, advocates of child liberation theology argue. In addition, the Bible does not direct parents to use corporal punishment to discipline children, though Christians have largely insisted otherwise. Proverbs 13:24 states, "He who spares the rod hates his son, but he who loves him is diligent to discipline him" (RSV). This statement refers to the rod used to herd sheep to guide and protect them from danger. The rod was not used to hit the sheep, and Psalm 23 makes the protective nature of the rod clear when it mentions that "thy rod and thy staff, they comfort me" (v. 4 RSV). As former social worker and Sunday school teacher Guida C. Eldorado explained in the *Chicago Tribune*,

> "Sparing the rod" . . . means that a parent must guide his or her child and teach the child right from wrong. The word "discipline" comes from the same root word as "disciple," and discipline is teaching, training, setting an example of proper behavior, and giving consequences that help a child learn how to behave better. The word "punish" comes from a root word that means to inflict physical pain. Furthermore, nowhere in the New Testament does Jesus tell parents to use corporal punishment with their children.[24]

Supporters of child liberation theology say that corporal punishment should be considered a "sinful practice." They cite research finding that more than a quarter of American children are hit hard enough by caregivers to sustain injuries and that harsh physical discipline increases the risk of a child developing heart disease, arthritis, obesity, mental disorders, and other problems once they become adults. Also compelling is that no evidence suggests corporal punishment improves a child's behavior. Rather, the more severely children are disciplined, the more likely they are to struggle with depression, anxiety, rage, and troubled relationships in the future.

hooks suffered from depression and suicidal ideation throughout her life, demonstrating the long-lasting effects of physical and emotional abuse. But in *Bone Black*, she describes how both her spiritual practice and the written word intersect to give her a sense of self-worth. Gloria takes comfort in praise and worship as a small child, and her faith identity only grows stronger and more complex during her teenage years. Family and community members show Gloria how they approach religion in vastly different ways. Some of her relatives present themselves as strict Christians but are unkind to Gloria and her siblings, and others are consistently kind in and out of church. She also has family members who are spiritual but wary of organized religion, preferring time in nature to attending worship services.

Although Gloria attends a Baptist church, she is exposed to other denominations and practices during her youth. She learns about Catholicism and Indigenous and Black American folk traditions, all of which shape the adult she becomes. While the Black church is the foundation for her spiritual practice, she ignores the idea that it must be the only tradition she follows. The Black church, though, plays a pivotal role in Gloria's development as a speaker and writer. Her appreciation for worship songs ignites her interest in the written word, as does reciting Scripture during church services.

Still, even as a small child, Gloria recognizes religion's flaws. She observes how sexism, classism, and racism influence what happens inside church walls.

LEARNING FROM BLACK BELIEVERS AND THE BLACK CHURCH

As a youngster growing up in rural, racially segregated Kentucky, Gloria doesn't understand that living in the sticks means she's poor. She's equally unaware that the reason the school bus picks up some children in her community and not others is based on race. Instead of taking the bus to school, the Watkins children walk about four miles roundtrip each weekday, rain or shine, to get an education. They are lucky, as some of their classmates must walk for much longer to reach the school for Black students.

Although just making it to school is often an ordeal for Gloria, once she arrives, she enjoys "the happiest moment of the day"—singing during morning chapel.[25] She doesn't understand every word in "Red River Valley," a folk song they sing, but the yearning it evokes resonates with her. The singing and the recitation of the Lord's Prayer are the beginning of her romance with poetry, with language overall.

Her burgeoning love for words also reveals itself at her family church, where Gloria performs in the children's choir. The choir sits away from the congregation, allowing her to look out into the pews and observe how the church recognizes the social status of members. She notices how the women of the church wear fancy, elaborate hats and how the congregants make sure to reserve a third pew seat for one hat wearer in particular: Miss Erma, a church founder. Gloria notices Miss Erma not only because of her funny, feathered hats but also because she is old, "older than we can imagine."[26] In addition, she notices the elderly woman because of the words Miss Erma belts out when moved by the preacher's sermon. "In a loud and piercing voice," Miss Erma thanks God, thanks Jesus, for "heartfelt religion."[27]

Although Gloria pays a great deal of attention to the old woman with the cane and the funny hat, she does not realize that Miss Erma has taken note of her, too. When Gloria begins to recite the Scripture for the morning offering—"my voice rising softly above the click of coins, the organ music, like smoke drifting and settling"[28]—the church elder approaches to let her know that she's been watching her grow up and is impressed by her Scripture reading. By doing so, Miss Erma becomes one of the first people to affirm Gloria as an orator. Afterward, she compensates Gloria for her talent. Gloria recalls,

> She waited for me after church, to hold me in those arms, to tell me
> that my reading (like the preacher's sermon) also found its way into the

heart, also pressed itself into the beating. Because of this she wanted to give me something, some gesture of her confidence that the god voice that came out of me and touched her beating heart would go on speaking and name itself in this world. She tells me to tell my mama to send me to her house. I become a regular visitor. Never allowed to stay long—only as long as it takes to speak a little, to be handed the gift, the gesture of her regard, I return home soon.[29]

Gloria cherishes the presents that Miss Erma gives to her. Sometimes, they come in boxes, other times in baskets or sacks. These gifts are so precious to Gloria that she never opens them until she reaches home and can share the "mysterious" tokens with her family. But the role Miss Erma plays in Gloria's life is far more important than gift giver. Miss Erma appreciates Gloria in a way those in the young girl's home do not. There, Gloria is routinely disciplined for talking back, and her voice results in her being labeled a problem child. To Miss Erma, however, Gloria has a "god voice" that touches her in the same way that the preacher's voice does. Just as child liberation theologians argue that children are as valuable as adults, Miss Erma regards Gloria's way with words as highly as she does the pastor's sermon. Moreover, she makes the crucial decision to tell Gloria this. Her gifts to Gloria aren't simply tokens of appreciation but serve to remind the youngster to put her speaking and reading skills to good use.

As a child subjected to physical, emotional, and verbal abuse as well as poverty, discrimination, and domestic violence, Gloria endures adverse childhood experiences (ACEs)—"potentially traumatic events that occur before a child reaches the age of 18."[30] According to the Centers for Disease Control and Prevention, ACEs make youth vulnerable to developing chronic health problems, mental illness, and substance use problems well into adulthood. They may negatively affect young people's academic and career trajectories as well.

Women and people of color disproportionately have multiple ACEs, but at-risk groups may also have protective factors that counteract the effects of ACEs and foster resilience. A relationship with a caring adult outside one's family is an example of a protective factor. Miss Erma stands out as one such adult in Gloria's child-hood. Having identified Gloria's talent as a reader and speaker, Miss Erma makes her feel that she is a special child and not the crazy, disobedient girl family members deem her to be. In this way, the elderly woman follows Jesus's example, treating Gloria with the compassion that he extended to children and not as a nuisance like his disciples did.

During a 2014 discussion at Eugene Lang College, hooks discussed the importance of adults affirming the creativity of the children in their lives:

> Get to know a child [so] that you can nurture their artistic practice, even if you only see that child for a half an hour.... There's a little Black girl I only see ... when her mother comes to braid my hair, but I make sure that there's something in that space that addresses her creativity, her beauty.... [Psychologist] Alice Miller talked about the fact that you can save a child by being that enlightened witness, and it doesn't have to be a constant thing, but who knows what can happen in that magical moment...that says, "You're beautiful. You're creative." And we can do that with Black children and other groups of children who are where we are.[31]

I can attest that hooks lived out this message. After hooks visited my school, I learned that she made a major impression on a student with whom I was friendly—a cute Black girl with short, relaxed hair. The girl disclosed that hooks told her that she was beautiful and sug-gested that she wear her hair natural. This acquaintance excitedly repeated this conversation to everyone in our circle. "bell hooks said I was beautiful!" And soon after, she stopped straightening her hair for good. In one conversation, hooks affirmed the beauty of a dark-skinned Black girl who sorely needed the message and challenged her to embrace her kinks and coils.

In *Bone Black*, be it during morning chapel at school or her family church, Gloria finds a space where she experiences enjoyment, nur-tures her love of language, and connects with people who observe and celebrate her talent. Having started her first book on feminism, *Ain't I a Woman*, when she was just nineteen, her affirming experiences in religious settings gave her the confidence early on to conceive of herself as a gifted writer, reader, and thinker.

Although Miss Erma distinguishes herself as one of *Bone Black*'s benevolent adults, another woman makes Gloria and her siblings feel small. Aunt Charley, their father's sister, is a widow no longer interested in romantic relationships with men, as she's "mainly concerned with god, piano music, and her beauty parlor business."[32] A legalistic Christian, Charley does not allow gossip in her parlor. None of the customary laughter or banter found in Black salons can be heard in the parlor that she operates from her kitchen. Instead, silence fills the business—with some exceptions. On occasion, the women chat about how impressed they are by the latest church sermon, but the salon is usually quiet other than discussions about religion. It's a dispiriting experience for a bookish girl like Gloria who is drawn to lively discussion.

Gloria helps at her aunt's salon to earn extra cash, but she doesn't enjoy the work or Charley. She does, however, become enchanted by the bars of Ivory soap at her aunt's house. In the Watkins household, everyone uses lye soap, which "comes in thick brown pieces that look more like stones than something one would use to wash the body."[33] Gloria and her siblings declare that they will not use lye soap when they grow up, unaware that their parents stock their household with the soap because they get it for free from their grandmother.

"We will have the best, only the sweet smelling," the Watkins children say of soap. But Gloria declares that she "will have only this milky white Ivory Soap,"[34] as its subtle fragrance does not trigger her to have an asthma attack as aggressively scented items do. That Ivory does not have an overpowering smell makes it particularly special to Gloria, but Aunt Charley never offers any of her brother's children a bar. In fact, she makes them wash their hands in a part of the house away from the customers and her Ivory stockpile. "Everything in her house is arranged to remind you that it is hers," writes hooks, a casual indictment of her aunt's character.[35]

In contrast, Gloria feels welcome at Miss Erma's house, which has cool, clean air that grazes her skin "like feathers" when she crosses the threshold. The spotless home reminds her of "bright new pennies."[36] Compare this to the stinginess and domination that Gloria experiences in her aunt's home. She notices how Aunt Charley makes "customers pay cash on the spot,"[37] limits what they can talk about, and dismisses their folk traditions.

Like Miss Erma, Aunt Charley enjoys class privilege that the Watkins family lacks. Along with her salon business, the widow drives a big car. While Miss Erma is generous with her gifts and her praise, however, Charley is short on both. Aunt Charley not only declines to offer the Watkins kids Ivory soap, she also constantly criticizes how Gloria performs chores. Much like Gloria feels powerless at her colorist grandmother's house, she feels slighted and repressed in her aunt's home. Charley and Erma may both be known as pious women, but only one of them exhibits Jesus's kindness.

While her father's sister is an uncharitable Christian, Gloria encounters several other believers who exude compassion. Some of these Christians are elderly men, who provide a gentle example of masculinity that contrasts completely with her father's violence and domination. Of these men, hooks says,

> They talked to her as if they understood one another, as if they were the same—nothing standing between them, not age, not sex. They were the brown-skinned men with serious faces who are the deacons of the church, the right-hand men of God. They were the men who wept when they felt his love, who wept when the preacher spoke of the good and faithful servant. They pulled wrinkled handkerchiefs out of their pockets and poured tears in them, as if they were pouring milk into a cup. She wanted to drink those tears that like milk would nourish her and help her grow.[38]

Gloria especially bonds with one such man, a deacon who has a disability. He reads the Scripture that accompanies the main offering, but his voice sounds wrinkled, and she struggles to understand most of his words except for the part discussing that "a man be found faithful."[39] She believes he says that part clearly because he is one of the faithful. After church, she always stands near him, grasping his hand until he must beg for it back in a pretend tearful voice. During these exchanges, he tells her about the country house he's been build-ing for years. One day, she finally visits the house, which makes her laugh because it is only half-built, and she doesn't understand how anyone can live in a half-built home. She senses that he's lonely, that the disability that causes him to hunch over has alienated him from the other adults in the community. She peppers him with questions about his disability and his personal life, and he takes in the little girl's questions with Christ-like patience.

Like Miss Erma, he also practices child liberation theology, treat-ing the young Gloria like an equal and receiving her as Christ did despite her stream of intrusive inquiries. While Gloria perceives that he's lonely, as an abused child, she is also lonely and alienated. In her household, probing questions result in her being beaten or otherwise disciplined, but in the deacon's half-built property, she has found refuge, a place she can ask anything without fear of reprisal.

In her maternal grandfather, Daddy Gus, Gloria finds another faithful man, another "right-hand [man] of god."[40] The family scape-goat, she is a youth in mourning, but he comforts her as Christ says in the Beatitudes that the grieving will be. Daddy Gus understands how marginalized she feels in her household and assures her that she will ultimately be all right. "What have they been doing to you now?" he asks her. Gloria appreciates his concern. "He knows that I am a wounded animal," she writes, "that they pour salt in the open sores just to hear me moan."[41] Gus also tells Gloria his secrets. His family members dismiss him as a collector of junk, but the old man is a Shintoist of sorts, confiding in Gloria that he believes "everything has life, a tiny soul inside it—things like pocketknives, coins, bits of ribbon."[42]

Daddy Gus influences her future as a storyteller, writer, and cul-tural critic by advising her to listen to the stories that objects tell her. He shows her the collection of notebooks he uses to jot down memories with his "secret pencil." In him, Gloria has an early writ-ing role model.

Daddy Gus also contributes to her development as a nonviolent feminist and anticapitalist believer. He tells her that he resents what the world offers to men, namely nonstop work and war. His sons who fought in wars are all damaged, but he refused to serve. A pacifist who is unafraid to stand up for his beliefs, he grows indignant when Gloria asks him why no one made him join the armed forces during wartime. "He tells me that no one can make you do anything against your will," hooks writes.[43]

Although Gloria respects her grandfather, other family members do not, particularly her father. In 2015 hooks said that because Daddy Gus was peaceful, her own father viewed him as less than, as "not good enough." She recalled, "My dad hated him. He dogged him out. . . . What I most remember about my Daddy Gus is how peaceful he was, how good he always was, that he never had a harsh word to say. My father thought, 'That's weak.'"[44]

But from Daddy Gus, Gloria drew strength. He gave her the courage to live authentically and recognize her self-worth. From him, she learned that she didn't need to conform.

CHAPTER THREE

Christianity for the Outcast

In *Bone Black*, Gloria desperately needs a man like Daddy Gus in her life. Unlike her father, Daddy Gus's presence teaches Gloria that "all men are not terrible, are not to be feared."[1] But Daddy Gus is not the only believer who stands out in hooks' memoir, for all the faithful men and women who bond with her deviate from the norm.

Daddy Gus is a pacifist, activist, and animist; the church deacon has a disability; and the book implies that Miss Erma is a lesbian or, at least, perceived to be one. When Gloria's parents accuse her of having a same-sex romance with her classmate, "they think about the way a certain funny grown-up woman showed intense interest in her," hooks writes. "They think that maybe they were wrong to allow her to accept presents, a dress, a watch with tiny diamonds."[2] Miss Erma is the likely culprit, as she is the only woman in the book described as giving Gloria presents and lavishing attention on her. That she is called "Miss Erma" and not "Mrs. Erma" indicates that she never married, which might have fueled speculation about her sexual orientation and be why Gloria is "never allowed" to visit her house for long.[3]

The outsider status of Miss Erma, the disabled deacon, and Daddy Gus gives each of them the empathy missing from a conformist and capitalist Christian like Aunt Charley. They know what it's like to be different and, as a result, offer Christlike compassion to a young

Gloria sorely in need of encouragement. Exposed to Christ's love through this trio and through her own relationship with the Lord, Gloria becomes emotional when she gives her life to him during her baptism. On this occasion, the words that have defined her spiritual practice fail her. She has relished reading the Scripture for the church offering and singing in the children's choir and in morning chapel at school, but when the preacher asks Gloria if she wants Jesus to be her personal savior, she struggles to speak. Gloria recalls,

> All the lines she had rehearsed, the pretty words that would describe her nightly meeting with God, their walks in the garden, the waiting for him near bushes of pink and white baby roses, the moist dew that sometimes caught in her hair, the way he warmed her hands with breath that smelled of honeysuckle and jasmine—all the words would not come. In place of words she gave them tears, the same tears that had wet his wounds, that like warm summer rain had caressed his flesh with everlasting love.[4]

Words fail her because her spiritual practice has been intimate and relational. Among an unfamiliar crowd in a public space, she can't bring herself to discuss her personal connection to God. But her tears are real, "holy,"[5] she calls them, for they symbolize her own heartfelt religion. She has no doubt that she wants to be a "bride of god,"[6] but she feels that giving herself to him during a public ceremony is a betrayal. She wonders if God will recognize her in the head-to-toe white clothes she has to wear for the ritual. Still, she goes forward with the baptism, concerned that it will bring an end to "all the private love" she has shared with the Lord.[7]

Her spiritual practice may be authentic, but Gloria questions certain church traditions. She notices that women can preach the gospel at the tent meetings the evangelical churches host. In her Baptist church, though, she learns that women may not preach, "were not worthy enough to even cross the threshold of god's anointed space—the pulpit."[8] This makes her feel that her femaleness precludes her from true holiness. She longs to attend a church where women may preach. She seeks out a tent meeting for this very experience but is disappointed to arrive and discover that the preacher is a man.

She knows that some men in the church, pastors and congregants alike, are hypocrites. When her father is baptized—an individual hooks describes in *Feminism Is for Everybody* as a "military man, an athlete, a deacon of the church, a provider, a womanizer . . . the embodiment of patriarchal rule"[9]—she does not rejoice. Instead, she questions if the baptism will really take, if the "water will betray him,"[10] suspicious that he's beyond redemption. On less significant occasions, she hears adults casually discussing deceitful pastors, "how they stand right up there in the pulpit and lie."[11] That a man of God would lie confuses Gloria and her siblings, but it doesn't stop them from trying to be true Christians themselves, for they know that "god loves the truth."[12]

On communion Sundays, she hears truth in the voices of the elderly women in her church. They sing with no accompaniment, keeping alive "the old ways."[13] Their voices are strong as they engage in call and response, a musical tradition that contains two related phrases—the latter serving as a comment in some way on the former. Common throughout the African diaspora, call and response is an oral tradition that fosters dialogue and encourages communal participation. It is a practice that by its nature opposes domination, and Gloria loves hearing the women sing.

She, too, puts her voice to use. She sings to institutionalized women and children as part of her youth missionary work, distressed to see people locked away without windows and air circulation. Although Gloria has trouble breathing in this environment, she tries her best to entertain the charges. She and the other young missionaries sing and dance until performing saps all their energy. She objects to the institutionalization of people with mental and physical disabilities, aware that in her rural, Black community, families take care of such individuals. Community members recognize the humanity of the disabled, and they don't need to undertake official mission work to do so.[14]

Gloria's Christian outreach does not stop there. After her mother buys her a book of religious stories, Gloria decides to share it with the "invalids and shut-ins" in her neighborhood.[15] It is her first new book—again linking her interest in literature with religion—and she goes from home to home reading the book to the vulnerable. When she receives a used book collection from a retired schoolteacher in her community, Gloria is even more overjoyed. The collection includes the works of women writers such as the Bronte sisters, Emily Dickinson, and George Eliot, along with male authors such as William Shakespeare, Charles Dickens, and Edgar Allan Poe. The books keep her company just as she provides company to her shut-in neighbors by reading to them.

But being a missionary is the one part of being a Christian that Gloria dislikes. She realizes that she prefers reading alone to going door-to-door reading to ailing community members. Like her relationship with Jesus, reading is intimate for her.

Gloria's disinterest in missionary work and desire to see women church leaders is not the only way she departs from traditional Christianity. She insists on believing in the African American folk traditions of her ancestors, the folk magic that her Aunt Charley calls "nonsense."[16] But in her maternal grandmother Saru—Sarah Hooks Oldham—Gloria finds an elder who has a spiritual practice that does not conform to institutional religion.

BEYOND ORGANIZED RELIGION

Saru is an old woman who practices the old ways. Of African American and Native American heritage, she makes quilts, lye soap, butter, and wine. She interprets dreams, wrings the necks of chickens, and stores her food in a pantry instead of a refrigerator. She tells Gloria that she can remember when Black people still spoke their ancestral languages and discussed their ancestral homelands. They only stopped talking about Africa because white people didn't want them to maintain a connection to their roots. But Saru feels that "a person cannot feel right in their heart if they have denied parts of their ancestral past."[17] She relays this message to Gloria because she wants her young granddaughter to pass these stories on; she believes Gloria is a maker of stories, words, and a "new fire."[18]

Although Saru does not read or write, she is yet another caring adult in Gloria's life who urges her to dedicate herself to words. Through the oral tradition and quiltmaking, the elderly woman is a storyteller, too. In *Yearning: Race, Gender, and Cultural Politics*, hooks discusses how her maternal grandmother's quilts had a narrative that began as soon as Saru (also called Baba) considered making one. "The story was rooted in the quilt's history, why it was made, why a particular pattern was chosen," hooks explains. "The story of a given quilt was central to Baba's creative self-expression, as family historian, storyteller, exhibiting the work of her hands."[19]

Saru is also a financial, spiritual, and feminist role model. In *Bone Black*, Gloria describes how her mother increasingly becomes cash conscious and loathes "the old ways,"[20] but Saru does not depend on store-bought items to survive. Rather, she values the ability to grow her own food and produce other vital resources independently. Her approach to religion is inspirational, too. She tells her granddaughter that "believing in God has nothing to do with going to church" and repeats the story of how she stopped attending services when she found out that the congregants "were more concerned with talking about what you were wearing and who you were with."[21] The story of how Saru left organized religion becomes one of Gloria's favorites. In this grandmother, Gloria finds "a woman of spirit, a woman of strong language, a fighter."[22] Gloria is viewed as a problem by her family for having too much spirit, but Saru's example reassures her that one can be a spirited woman and have a fulfilling existence.

Saru views herself as a "child of the outdoors" and a "wild and untamed" woman.[23] In this way, she mirrors the fictionalized wild women that Morrison describes in books such as *The Bluest Eye*, *Song of Solomon*, *Beloved*, and *Paradise*. hooks found Morrison's literature to be life-changing because she saw herself in the characters, but she also would have seen the lives of women like Saru represented on the pages. Usually elderly, these women buck gender norms, worship on their own terms, and have the capacity to heal both the mind and the spirit.

Quiltmaking is one way that Saru nurtures her spirit. In *Yearning*, hooks recalls how her grandmother considered that craft to be a spiritual process.

> It was a form of meditation where the self was let go. This was the way she had learned to approach quiltmaking from her mother. To her it was an art of stillness and concentration, a work which renewed the spirit. Fundamentally, in Baba's mind quiltmaking was women's work, an activity that gave harmony and balance to the psyche. According to her, it was that aspect of a country woman's work which enabled her to cease attending to the needs of others and "come back to herself." It was indeed "rest for the mind."[24]

From Saru, Gloria learns how rural Black women approach meditative spiritual practice. Later, this exposure will serve her well as a Buddhist, a spiritual practice that emphasizes self-actualization, a development that occurs when a person releases the idea of self. Saru is a self-actualized woman, whether she is growing food, telling stories, opposing classism in the church, or nurturing her spirituality through quiltmaking. By watching Saru dedicate herself to the quiltmaking craft until old age prevents her from doing so, Gloria learns to commit herself to the writing craft.

Changing times and textiles do not deter Saru from quiltmaking, and she is not the only community member attached to the old ways. In Aunt Charley's salon, many of the customers practice African American folk traditions. They put their shorn locks in brown paper sacks, and some plan to burn their cut hair because they believe it will help the hair left on their heads grow faster. Other clients are careful to confiscate their cut hair before leaving the salon to prevent it from getting into the hands of harm-doers. Gloria and her siblings agree that many magical practices can be conducted with hair, but Aunt Charley ridicules traditions rooted in African American folk magic.

"We know not to believe her," hooks writes. "We know magic is real. We take all the hair and put it in the trash. It will all be burned."[25]

While Gloria does not use the term *hoodoo* to describe this magic, the practices she describes fall into this category of spiritual practice. In *Mojo Workin': The Old African American Hoodoo System*, Katrina Hazzard-Donald defines hoodoo as "the indigenous, herbal, healing, and supernatural-controlling spiritual folk tradition of the African American in the United States."[26] Also known as conjure, rootwork, and spirit work, "hoodoo," she writes, "for African Americans, is embodied historical memory linking them back through time to previous generations and ultimately to their African past. It is also a paradigm for approaching both the world and all areas of social life."[27]

For generations, African American parents, grandparents, and great-grandparents have passed on hoodoo-related spiritual practices to the younger people in their lives. As Saru does with Gloria, sometimes they make a concerted effort to pass on these details, and other times, they transmit this information because it is an integral part of their daily routines. In any case, hoodoo is designed to help African Americans successfully confront the problems they face in everyday life, be it revenge against their oppressors, luck finding work, or a remedy for an illness. Having been described as both Black American "indigenous medicine" and "psychiatry,"[28] hoodoo is also designed to address the conflicts that arise in interpersonal relationships, especially involving lovers, romantic rivals, and enemies generally.

At Aunt Charley's beauty salon, the customers worry that one of their nemeses might use their cut hair to curse them. But by reducing these concerns to "nonsense," Charley overlooks the long and complex role that hoodoo has played in Black American life.

During a 2015 discussion, hooks lamented that Christianity disconnected her family members from African-derived folk traditions. Saru might have clung to the old ways, but other relatives distanced themselves from spiritual practices such as hoodoo. hooks remarked,

> One of the things that I most admire about our ancestors was their capacity to develop oppositional thinking. As Black people like my parents became more Christian, they dropped oppositional thinking.

No more reading of dreams. No more going to the person who is a psychic. Christianity really attacked all of that in the freed slaves and ancestors.[29]

Sometimes described as "the devil's work," as those of European descent routinely demonized African-origin practices, hoodoo is a tradition that has occasionally been framed as opposing Christianity. Historically, however, hoodoo practitioners overwhelmingly identified as Christians, incorporating the Psalms and other Scriptures into their rootwork. Hazzard-Donald notes that hoodoo is even found in Black church traditions such as the ring shout, a sacred dance ritual. During the ring shout, churchgoers step in a counterclockwise motion, typically praising the Lord while doing so. Although *shout* is in the name, the ring shout does not require participants to actually yell out. The "shout" in this practice is said to derive from the Afro-Arabic word *saut*, a term for the ritual dance performed around "the House of God," or the Kaaba, in Mecca, Saudi Arabia.[30] The holy city is the destination where Muslims are required to make a pilgrimage at least once in their lives.

In *Bone Black*, Gloria describes seeing the ring shout during visits to country churches. In them, she sees "overweight ladies faint" and "folk just [going] wild with religion—singing, shouting, praying, praising the lord all over the place."[31] Shouting is an abbreviated colloquialism for the ring shout.

Intertwined with Black church tradition, hoodoo is also likely a product of the cultural exchanges between African Americans and Native Americans. After they were held captive and forced to cross the Atlantic, West and Central Africans brought with them to the United States extraordinary agricultural prowess, their genius revealed by the many crops that thrived under their care. But encounters with Indigenous Americans, well versed in the local plants of the land, may have enhanced their existing agricultural knowledge and informed how they practiced herbalism under a hoodoo framework.[32] Those of mixed Black and Native American heritage would have been primed to combine practices from both groups while cultivating crops or concocting herbal remedies.

Influenced by Native American and African American approaches to life, Saru is one such person in *Bone Black*. With her as a role model, Gloria holds on to the folk magic of her elders, paying close attention to her dreams and keeping the hair of Aunt Charley's customers out of the hands of possible foes.

Saru's syncretic belief system and insistence that one needn't go to church to be a believer paves the way for Gloria to fashion a unique spiritual identity of her own as an adult—Buddhist Christian. As a youth, she is not closed off to spiritual traditions outside the Black Baptist church. She becomes involved in both the campus ministry of her racially integrated high school and a religious tradition she finds altogether mysterious, Catholicism. Diversifying the spiritual modalities in her life proves to be a lifesaving move for the teenager.

CAMPUS CRUSADE AND CATHOLICISM

As a youth, Gloria connects with several people who serve as sources of support or "enlightened witnesses" in her life—her maternal grandparents, church elders, and even caring teachers—but she does not emerge from childhood unscathed. Her traumatic childhood causes her to turn inward the hostility and harmful scripts she receives from her immediate family members. Routinely melancholy, her resolve to live weakens, but she has a dream that leads to her spiritual awakening.

In the dream, Gloria and Daddy Gus enter a cave "covered with paintings that describe the way each animal has come to know that inside all of us is a place for healing."[33] The catch is that everyone has to discover this place of healing on their own. In the cave, Gloria and Daddy Gus feel peace; they feel free to lose themselves in sorrow. They then make a fire that contains all the lost spirits that show them how to live in the world. While Gloria does not know how to communicate with the spirits, her wise grandfather, who is sure that every object has a soul, can speak with them. Once outside the cave, Daddy Gus tells Gloria that, though the wisdom of the cave is available to all, she must not share its knowledge with anyone who isn't an authentic truth seeker.

A genuine seeker herself, she honors that agreement but captures her dream about the cave in a painting after learning the term *bone black*: "a black carbonaceous substance obtained by calcifying bones in closed vessels."[34] The description of the color makes her think of burning bones, "flesh on fire, turning black, turning into ash."[35] Saru has already told her that it is Gloria's heart that burns in the center of the flames, that her troubled granddaughter is "making the new fire."[36] In the end, Gloria's painting, *Autumn in the Wilderness*, depicts the cave, the fire inside, the lost spirits, and the animals sacrificed "to keep the spirit moving, burning bright."[37] She paints the bottom of the fire the darkest hue, *bone black*.

While attempting to perfect the work, Gloria realizes that she is painting the wilderness in which her spirit roams. When she left the cave with Daddy Gus, she entered the wilderness. As a girl with too much spirit, she is wild like Saru and Bell Blair Hooks, the great-grandmother whose name she later assumed. But as an abused child, she must also take refuge in the wilderness like the women of the Bible who find themselves in similar circumstances. In the book of Genesis, Hagar runs into the wilderness after the couple who enslaves her forces her to bear their child, only to abuse her after she conceives. In the wilderness, Hagar encounters an angel of the Lord who tells her that "the Lord has heard [her] misery" and offers her reassurance. She will give birth to a "wild donkey of a man"—a man who will not live in bondage—the angel tells her.[38] And the number of her descendants will rival the stars in the sky. Though Hagar's life appears to be bleak, the angel informs her that she will emerge from the wilderness triumphant.

Hagar's story has been an inspiration to abused, enslaved, and oppressed women in need of hope that God sees them. According to CBE International, which advocates for egalitarianism for women and men in the church,

> Hagar's story is more than the story of a slave and her son. It is a story of God's care for those who have no earthly hope. On the heels of

miserable treatment, perhaps at the hands of pious and religious people, abuse victims may be amazed to realize that they are not alone after all. In their most trying hours, they may discover the Lord whispering to them by name, intimately concerned for them. When they suffer because of events beyond their control, when they are cast out, and when they give up on life itself, they may be shocked that God hears their cries. When they experience setbacks, it may delight them to know that the Lord walks the winding path of recovery with them, and has promised new life in Christ.[39]

After Gloria's autumn in the wilderness, she becomes involved in the campus ministry of her high school, the first integrated school she attends. Her activities in religious groups as a teenager and the encouragement of Daddy Gus—who hears the souls of "the treasures people have lost or abandoned . . . crying in the wilderness"[40]—lead her to understand that she is not alone. She is a treasure, and there is a place she belongs. She just needs to find it.

Taking part in the Campus Crusade for Christ sets her on the path toward healing, but she is slow to join the group because her spiritual vision conflicts with the ministry's basic tenets. She does not believe in one god, for example, but in all gods. She believes in evil but not in sin. Despite these major differences in belief, Gloria takes part in the campus ministry, experiencing the love of its members when they lay hands on her to stop her asthma attacks. Afterward, her asthma does not go away even though she believes in miracles and the power of touch. Still, she credits that night with making "all other nights of healing possible."[41]

At Campus Crusade gatherings, she is free to be herself, to discuss her anguish. At home, the opposite is true. Her family tires of her being "disconsolate," a new word they use to describe her.[42] They fear that her activities in the campus ministry are making her sadder rather than happier, ignoring how their chronic criticism and shaming affects her emotionally. Alienated in her household, Gloria feels a sense of belonging in Campus Crusade. When she and fellow members sing, eat, and hold hands together, she feels solace instead of the disconsolation she experiences in her high-conflict home. Going on a Campus Crusade retreat provides her with respite from the ongoing strife in her household. She writes,

> I am glad to be at the retreat, to escape the tensions of home, the feeling that I stand on the edge of a cliff about to fall off. I know that many people come to God to be rescued, to be taken from the cliff and placed on solid ground. I come to God and yet remain at the edge of the cliff. I have not been rescued. For comfort I read over and over the story of John the Baptist wandering in the wilderness. I too linger in the wilderness wanting desperately to find my way.[43]

John the Baptist was an outsider in his community. Dressed in a coarse camel's hair frock and a leather belt that call attention to "his preaching a baptism of repentance,"[44] he lived in the Judean wilderness, relying on God to provide locusts and honey for him to eat. Others thought of him as odd, not only because of the wild man's clothing and diet but also because John was a prophet and truth teller. From the wilderness, he called out the leaders of the organized church for their lust for power and abandonment of the oppressed. In the wilderness—where the Jews spent forty years and Jesus spent forty days—people experienced spiritual restoration. But to do so, they had to first confront the forces that alienated them from God. This was the repentance of John the Baptist, who spent much of his life alone in the wilderness but whose preaching reached the people, nonetheless. His ministry was thought of as "the voice of one crying in the wilderness."[45]

In her wilderness, in the darkness of the cave of her soul, Gloria is not alone but lonely. She longs for community, fearful that she will step off the metaphorical cliff in her mind and jump. She never says aloud that she wants to take her life, but she recognizes her suicidality. That changes during the Campus Crusade retreat, where she hears a Catholic priest give a sermon in which he states that loneliness and depression are normal. He, too, has experienced these emotional states without actively attempting to end his life. In awe that someone can relate to what she has experienced, a sobbing Gloria speaks with the priest when he finishes his sermon. He tells her that she "will overcome her fear and leap into life, that she will bring with her the treasures that are her being: the beauty, the courage, the wisdom." He says "to let that young woman into my heart to begin to love her so that she can live and live and go on living."[46]

Following their exchange, the priest sends a student to spend time with her at the retreat. The student gives Gloria a copy of Rainer Maria Rilke's *Letters to a Young Poet*. The 1929 collection of letters about poetry, love, and other topics helps Gloria make sense of her pain. She reads poetry and begins writing herself. She recites passages of *Letters to a Young Poet* to Daddy Gus, who tells her that one day she will no longer suffer and reassures her "there are lots of ways to belong in this world" when she confides in him how much it hurts to be an outsider.[47]

Writing, she realizes, is her destiny. In the darkness of her bedroom at night, she tries to find her way to her spiritual home. In the bone black cave, she creates a space where she belongs. She fits into the world of words, in the stories she tells, the poems she writes, and the dreams she records. She has a home.

Without the enlightened witnesses in her life and the spiritual traditions they expose her to, Gloria might not have found her way home. In morning chapel at her grade school and in her family church, she develops a love for the sung, spoken, and written word. Miss Erma encourages her to nurture her talent, her "god voice." The deacon allows her to ask him question after question about his life and disability, prompting him to tell his own stories and abating his loneliness as he does hers. Daddy Gus and Saru encourage her to be a storyteller by advising her to listen to the stories of the objects around her and informing her that words are her destiny. Even her mother, with whom she is often at odds, encourages her by buying her a book of religious stories.

Throughout her youth, Gloria's love of words intersects directly with her spiritual practice. But before she can experience the spiritual awakening she has at the end of *Bone Black*, Gloria must learn to love herself, the girl her father thinks has too much spirit. She must recognize that she fits somewhere, even as she feels "excommunicated"[48] by her immediate family members.

Gloria realizes that she belongs on the page, but she would not have had that revelation without the circle of faithful people—church and unchurched, Protestant and Catholic, Black and white, male and female—who affirm her. With their help, she develops a spiritual vision that opposes racism, sexism, and classism and is heavily influenced by the Black church but open to the teachings of different faiths. "To us the Catholic church is a mystery," hooks writes.[49] But it is a white Catholic priest who lets Gloria know that she is not alone in her suffering, that despite it, she must learn to love herself.

In arranging for her to read *Letters to a Young Poet*, a book Rilke wrote after receiving countless requests for advice from young people in distress, the priest demonstrates once again that he sees Gloria. Seen by the priest and by the enlightened witnesses who come before him, particularly Saru and Daddy Gus, Gloria finally sees herself.

CHAPTER FOUR

A Feminist Approach to Spirituality

In both her church and her campus ministry, Gloria Jean Watkins learned to love and accept herself despite growing up in a household where she perpetually felt rejected. By adulthood, she'd gained the confidence to pursue a career as a writer and a scholar, fashioning a new identity—bell hooks—for herself in the process. In *Feminism Is for Everybody*, hooks' 2000 primer on the women's liberation movement, she reveals that achieving self-love and self-acceptance was critical to her personal development, as she would not have become a fully realized person without them.

When hooks first took part in the feminist movement as a college student in the 1970s, she also learned about the importance of loving herself. In consciousness-raising groups, feminists sought to heal themselves from the "patriarchal assaults" they experienced in their families of origin or intimate relationships.[1] In these therapeutic feminist circles, women were affirmed spiritually and emotionally. Perhaps because the message she received about self-love and self-acceptance in religious environments and in feminist circles echoed each other, she did not view being a feminist of faith as a contradiction. In fact, she argues in her primer, "Feminism has been and continues to be a resistance movement which valorizes spiritual practice."[2]

BELL HOOKS' SPIRITUAL VISION

Feminists of the nineteenth and early twentieth centuries led the modern spiritualism movement while advancing causes such as women's suffrage and the abolition of slavery. Their counterparts in the 1960s, '70s, and '80s practiced what hooks calls "creation spirituality" or "goddess-centered spirituality,"[3] types of neopaganism also embraced by twenty-first-century feminists fighting for equal pay, reproductive rights, and an end to sexual violence. Those gender equality advocates involved in organized religion championed feminist, womanist, and mujerista theologies to highlight the role of women in such traditions.

No matter the time period, women who've fought for gender, racial, economic, or LGBTQ+ equality have paired their activism with spiritualities that honor the sacred feminine. They understood that empowerment in both the sociopolitical and spiritual realms is necessary for women to realize their human potential. This recognition led feminists to reject or reinterpret religions that suggest women are inherently evil, deceitful, or inferior to men.

hooks was one such feminist. She sought out the divine feminine in Buddhism and Christianity alike. Having encouraged women to leave fundamentalist religions, she embraced the mystical Christianity and African-derived spirituality of her elders. But she also made a point to recognize the divinity of nature, revealing pagan inclinations. Women are served best, she believed, by practicing the traditions they connect to most. That's the case even if it means engaging in syncretism or blending religions together.

HONORING THE SACRED FEMININE

Historically, women have shown remarkable resilience as followers of religions that relegate them to the sidelines. In *Feminism Is for Everybody,* hooks notes that, for centuries, women have taken action to find "solace and sanctuary" in patriarchal religions. "Throughout the history of the church in Western life women have turned to monastic traditions to find a place for themselves where they can be with god without the intervention of men, where they can serve the divine without male domination."[4]

To back up her argument, hooks points to the English mystic Julian of Norwich, who lived during the Middle Ages from 1342 to about 1416. Although she is sometimes called Juliana of Norwich, Mother Julian, the Lady Julian, and Dame Julian, her real identity remains unknown. The name Julian refers to St. Julian's Church in Norwich, where the mystic known for her book, *Revelations of Divine Love,* spent most of her life as an anchoress—a woman cloistered in a cell to dedicate her days and nights to prayer and meditation. Julian is an historically important figure both because of her spiritual insight and because of the belief that she was the first woman to write a book in English.[5]

On May 8, 1373, a day she thought would be her last, an image of a bleeding Christ appeared before her. The sixteen visions Julian saw while believing she lay dying deepened her understanding of Christ, including his suffering and love for humanity. The experience inspired her to write *Revelations of Divine Love,* the book that is now considered a spiritual classic and has been cited by influential twentieth-century writers such as Iris Murdoch and T. S. Eliot.[6]

In this text, Julian trusts God while exploring doubt and fear from a theological perspective. Julian was a spiritual advisor to the people of Norwich, a community that endured famine, plague, and poverty during her lifetime. Her words comforted the suffering. For example, she writes in chapter 45 of *Revelations of Divine Love,* "Peace and love are always in us, being and working, but we are not always in peace and love. But he wants us to pay attention to this: that he is the foundation of our whole life in love."[7]

hooks was a youth when she first took an interest in exploring love through a spiritual and emotional lens, so her attraction to Julian of Norwich is hardly a mystery. But Julian's writing about divine love was not the only reason hooks felt drawn to her. The reclusive mystic's framing of divinity as feminine appealed to hooks as well. hooks explains,

> With keen spiritual insight and divine clarity the mystic Julian of Norwich would write long before the advent of contemporary feminism: "Our savior is our true mother in whom we are endlessly born

and out of whom we shall never come." Daring to counter the notion of our savior is always and only male Julian of Norwich was charting the journey back to the sacred feminine, helping to free women from the bondage of patriarchal religion.[8]

Using Julian as a model, hooks demonstrates how women of devout faith—Christian faith, at that—have longed to see themselves represented as divine. Before Christianity, agrarian societies worshipped ancient goddesses painted black, purportedly because the most fertile soil is the darkest in hue.[9] When Christianity spread, its leaders are said to have appropriated these images, giving rise to paintings of the Virgin Mary as dark-skinned. Imagery of the Black Madonna inspired hooks, who made a pilgrimage to the Shrine of the Black Madonna in Montserrat. Observing the statue "nourished my soul," hooks states in *Homegrown*. "This image of a beautiful, dark Madonna, blessing and healing the world, is counter hegemonic: It challenges the equation of Blackness with ugliness."[10]

The Shrine of the Black Madonna affirmed hooks' race and sex, allowing her to reimagine Christianity from a Black female perspective. The scholar's desire to engage a feminist spirituality was not unusual. In *Feminism Is for Everybody*, hooks describes how the second wave feminist movement that began in the 1960s and continued through the 1980s overlapped with a countercultural shift away from fundamentalist religion. This trend mirrored the spiritualist movement of the nineteenth century. Then, women's rights activists fighting for suffrage, property rights, and temperance (since alcoholic men often committed domestic violence or impoverished their families) turned increasingly to spiritualism, a Christian offshoot later deemed an independent religion. When the 1848 Seneca Falls Convention—the nation's first women's rights conference—took place, modern spiritualism was spreading throughout the United States.

Inspired by the ideas of eighteenth-century Swedish philosopher Emanuel Swedenborg, whose 1758 book *Heaven and Hell* explores the afterlife, the spiritualism movement was popularized by women such as the Fox Sisters, who (falsely) claimed the ability to communicate with a spirit in their Hydesville, New York, home.[11] Spiritualists believed that it was possible to communicate with the dead, a comforting notion during a time when many infants never made it out of childhood, women often died in childbirth, hundreds of thousands of men died during the Civil War, and people of all genders and ages were vulnerable to death by infectious disease.

When spiritualism took off in the mid-1800s, it became one of the limited avenues women had to speak in public. Feminists used the opportunity to advocate for women's rights and related causes. Spiritualism also gave them cover, as it was easy to blame their progressive politics on messages from spirits.

The spiritualism movement attracted many well-known followers, including Sir Arthur Conan Doyle, First Lady Mary Todd Lincoln, and Sojourner Truth, both a suffragist and an abolitionist.[12] The next wave of feminists did not become devoted spiritualists. However, as they explored solutions to gender inequality, they took an interest in alternative religion.

POLITICS AND PAGANISM

While nineteenth-century feminists championed spiritualism, second-wave feminists combined politics and paganism. Feminism's second wave—a term popularized by a March 1968 *New York Times Magazine* article called "The Second Feminist Wave: What Do These Women Want?"—aligned themselves with a variety of causes.[13] In addition to fighting for reproductive rights and an end to sexual violence, they demanded workplace and antidiscrimination protections. They drew attention to issues including sexuality, marriage, family life, and patriarchal dominance. Many of these women questioned the patriarchy in the Judeo-Christian tradition. They leaned toward New Age and Eastern spirituality and, to a lesser degree, Indigenous and traditional African religions.

In *Feminism Is for Everybody*, hooks recounts how a number of feminists felt emotionally connected to the female deities they encountered in Hinduism, Buddhism, and Vodou. Today, such women would likely face accusations of cultural appropriation, and, in fact, some of them were colonizing forces on these spiritual traditions—repackaging, marketing, and profiting off practices to which they had no ancestral connection by presenting themselves as experts. Some of these women, however, did have lineal ties to the religious traditions they began practicing, such as Black American women embracing West African spirituality or white American women embracing the paganism of Europe.

"For most of human history, God was present in everything, in animals, in plants, in men, in women, in all races," feminist leader Gloria Steinem said during a 1993 speech to commemorate the three hundredth anniversary of the Salem witch trials. "The word 'pagan' just means 'of nature.' It's supposed to be a terrible thing, of course, but that's all it means."[14]

For Starhawk—author of 1979's *The Spiral Dance: A Rebirth of the Ancient Religion of the Great Goddess*—learning about paganism as a first-year college student in the late 1960s was life changing. Born Miriam Simos, she took the name Starhawk as an adult after it came to her in a dream, explaining in 2004 that tradition dictates that "when you're initiated as a witch that you change your name."[15] Starhawk's journey to witchcraft was not linear but began while she was working on an anthropology project about witches with a classmate. As Starhawk researched, she discovered "that there was this whole theory about witches being the old pre-Christian pagan religions of Europe," she said in a 2022 podcast interview. "And now that seems pretty obvious, but at the time, that was a radical idea that there even were pre-Christian religions. And I just thought that was so exciting, and we just got totally into it. We formed a coven."[16]

Although she and her classmate went on to get training from actual witches, their interest in paganism waned eventually. Then came the women's liberation movement, renewing Starhawk's interest in earth-based religions and intensifying her belief that "there should be some connection between feminism and the religion of the Goddess."[17] Prior to her introduction to paganism, Starhawk had never considered that a deity could be anything other than male. As she explained during her podcast interview,

> I was raised Jewish and even though God was supposed to have no gender and no sex and no form, somehow he was always referred to as "he." And in Hebrew, the language is very, very gendered in a way English is not, where every verb changes according to whether you're female or male. So it was always in the male form for God. And the idea that you could see God in female form to me was just a radical and very empowering idea, a very affirming idea. Yes, women could actually take leadership because there weren't a lot of leadership roles in Judaism at that time. It was a few years before the feminist movement started inspiring women to say, "Hey, why shouldn't we be rabbis? Why shouldn't we be cantors?"[18]

In *The Spiral Dance*, an introduction to feminist witchcraft, Starhawk emphasizes the link between the divine feminine, Mother Earth, magic, and politics. She asserts that the feminist movement is not only political in nature but also magical and spiritual.

For Black feminists, most of whom grew up in church-going families like hooks did, religion and politics always complemented each other. The Black church, after all, birthed the civil rights movement and, before that, resistance movements against enslavement. Raised in communities where religion and activism had been braided together historically, Black feminists typically already had a politico-spiritual foundation when they joined the women's liberation struggle.

In her 1983 book, *In Search of Our Mothers' Gardens: Womanist Prose*, writer Alice Walker uses the term *womanism* to describe Black feminists and feminists of color. From the term *womanish*, which older generations of African Americans used to characterize girls who displayed "outrageous, audacious, courageous or willful behavior," womanists were feminists who had active spiritual lives, among other qualities. A womanist "loves the moon. Loves the spirit," Walker writes of them.[19]

hooks did not identify as a womanist. She argued that Black women didn't need a separate term to describe themselves in the feminist movement because the term she coined—"imperialist white supremacist capitalist patriarchy"—captured the interlocking forms of oppression that target them. But she also believed that it was important for feminists of different racial backgrounds to join in solidarity. During a 2015 discussion at Eugene Lang College, hooks said of womanism,

> There is no mass-based political movement in our society known as womanism. And there has never been. . . . I don't care how much Alice Walker talks about womanism; she [personally] developed within the framework of politicized feminism. . . . There continues to be a deep hatred between Black women and white women fueled by ongoing competition, fueled by one group feeling that as long as they are at the center, the other group has to be down under. And I think that to some extent, unfortunately, the womanism allowed Black women to feel like, "We got something better going on than white girls; we got womanism." But, in fact, it took us away from the political significance of what does it even take to build solidarity?[20]

hooks believed that it was more important to stand with women who have "dared to claim feminism" than to claim womanism.[21] In her dismissal of womanism in this instance, however, she suggested that the need some Black women have to separate themselves from the feminist movement is strictly rooted in mutual hatred or competition with white women. This stance ignores the Black women who felt that feminism didn't address their particular needs or those who experienced covert or overt anti-Black racism in the women's liberation movement and desired a space whether they would feel safe and seen.

The leaders of the first-wave feminist movement, at times, ignored the existence of Black women altogether. While meeting with abolitionist Frederick Douglass in 1866, women's rights activist Susan B. Anthony notoriously said, "I will cut off this right arm of mine before I will ever work or demand the ballot for the Negro and not the woman."[22] To Anthony's ilk, "woman" equaled white woman exclusively. This problem persisted during the second-wave feminist movement. Then, the National Organization for Women presented John Lennon and Yoko Ono with a "Positive Image of Women" honor for making a "strong pro-feminist statement" with their 1972 song "Woman Is the Nigger of the World," despite the title's use of a racial slur and implication that Black women, and the very real oppression they face, don't exist.[23]

Clearly, hooks was well versed in this history. She wrote *Ain't I a Woman* to illustrate how Black American women have been viciously oppressed because of their race and gender. In the book, she discusses historic fractures between white and Black women, arguing that nineteenth-century Christian fundamentalism led to the former attaining the status of goddess—"virtuous, pure, innocent, not sexual."[24] As the white woman was "mythologized" as a "symbolic Virgin Mary,"[25] Black women "were labeled jezebels and sexual temptresses and accused of leading white men away from spiritual purity into sin."[26] These stereotypes allowed white men to sexually brutalize enslaved Black women with abandon. She elaborates,

> Christian mythology depicted women as the source of sin and evil; racist-sexist mythology simply designated black women the epitome of female evil and sinfulness. White men could justify their dehumanization and sexual exploitation of black women by arguing that they possessed inherent evil demonic qualities. Black men could claim that they cannot get along with black women because they were so evil. And white women could use the image of the evil sinful black woman to emphasize their own innocence and purity. Like the biblical figure Eve, black women became the scapegoats for the misogynist men and racist women who needed to see some group of women as the embodiment of female evil.[27]

Typically, hooks writes, neither Black men nor white women came to the aid of Black women who had been sexually violated. Some white women even tormented sexually abused Black women who approached them for help. Others, she states, procured Black women for white male relatives solely to ensure these men would be sexually gratified.[28]

These horrific antebellum anecdotes point to a centuries-old lack of allyship between Black and privileged white women. And they continue to inform the present. A 2017 study published in the *Psychology of Women Quarterly* found that white female college students are less likely to intervene when their Black female peers are at risk for "incapacitated sexual assault."[29] This is yet another indication that conflicts between white and Black women don't merely stem from rivalry or mutual hatred but from many white women's lack of empathy for Black women and the resulting erasure of Black women's priorities from women's rights movements.

hooks herself acknowledged that "privileged white women often experience a greater sense of solidarity with men of their same class than with poor white women or women of color."[30] And during a 2014 New School appearance with Steinem, hooks spoke of the racial divide in the feminist movement more bluntly. Describing why Steinem's kindness and consideration to her stood out when they first met, hooks said, "Let's face it. Most white women feminists had not been kind to us Black women, women of color."[31]

At the bottom of the nation's social hierarchy, Black women are certainly not the group that believes that "as long as they are at the center, the other group has to be down under." For one, they are usually not centered in discussions about feminism, even in the twenty-first century. Far underrepresented in management and leadership roles with a long and traumatic history of performing domestic and slave labor, often for white women, Black women have been in no position to compete with their ruling class counterparts.

hooks may not have supported the use of the term *womanism*, but she was a woman who loved the spirit, just like the womanists of Walker's *In Search of Our Mothers' Gardens*. Also, in her feminist primer, hooks makes a point to mention not only the religious practices in which white women found belonging, but also Vodou, a tradition in which Black women have.

Luisah Teish, author of the 1985 book *Jambalaya: The Natural Woman's Book of Personal Charms and Practical Rituals*, sought to reclaim the term *Vodou*. In a 1987 interview, she said it meant "life force," "genius," or "protective spirit" and could be found in all West African–derived faith traditions of the Americas.[32] In *Jambalaya*, she calls Vodou "a science of the oppressed, a repository of womanknowledge."[33] Walker endorsed the book, describing it as a work "of startling remembrances, revelations, directives, and imperatives, filled with the mysticism, wisdom, and common sense of the African religion of the Mother."[34]

Teish started on the path of writing *Jambalaya* and becoming a Yoruba priestess in the 1970s, a period when she had also been politically active. She said that she could not separate her faith from her politics and that nature-based religions are liberatory because women see themselves represented as holy figures in ways they aren't in the Abrahamic faiths. In 1987, Teish said,

> I've seen many women injured by the patriarchal slant of religion and by the total imbalance in our society, and I know that the average woman lives in the shadow of a lifetime of negation. In order to heal that, it's necessary to give special attention to women, to highlight the feminine in everything. But it's also important not to create a universe that is lopsided in the other direction, in reaction to patriarchy. We've got to get rid of the arrogant notion that Mother Nature made a mistake when she made us different colors and sexes. We've got to stop saying that some of the mistakes we've made in human culture are "human nature." We've got to realize that it's too easy now to destroy each other, to indulge in negative tribalism.[35]

Teish was not a gender separatist, but she did want women to have a spirituality that exalted them rather than men exclusively. Several decades after *Jambalaya*'s release, the book remains popular with women interested in exploring the divine feminine. Just as Starhawk exposed a largely white female readership to the paganism of Europe through *The Spiral Dance*, Teish familiarized a largely women-of-color readership with traditional African religion through *Jambalaya*.

But as feminists like Starhawk and Teish celebrated the divine feminine in the 1970s and '80s, others distanced themselves from religion entirely. "Early on in feminist movement conflicts arose between those individual activists who felt the movement should stick to politics and take no stand on religion," hooks recalls in *Feminism Is for Everybody*. "A large number of the women who had come to radical feminism from traditional socialist politics were atheist. They saw efforts to return to a vision of sacred femininity as apolitical and sentimental."[36]

Divisions over the role of spirituality in feminism were short-lived, according to hooks, as even nonreligious feminists recognized that a liberatory spirituality could play a role in challenging faith-based patriarchy. More specifically, they knew that many of the nation's gender norms derived from Judeo-Christian religion. "Truly, there can be no feminist transformation of our culture without a transformation in our religious beliefs," hooks states in *Feminism Is for Everybody*.[37]

Despite the clear links between feminism and spirituality, the mainstream media has often been disinterested in documenting the connection between the two, hooks notes. As a result, the feminist movement is widely perceived to be an antireligious phenomenon focused exclusively on women's gains and civil rights. "In actuality feminism has helped transform patriarchal religious thought so that more women can find a connection to the sacred and commit to spiritual life," hooks writes.[38]

Although the news media overwhelmingly ignored the role that spirituality played in feminist circles, journalist Margot Adler did chronicle this trend in 1979's *Drawing Down the Moon: Witches, Druids, Goddess-Worshippers, and Other Pagans in America Today*, an exhaustive exploration of the US neopagan movement and for years the only introductory work on the topic. The seminal book on earth-based religions includes a chapter called "Women, Feminism, and the Craft." It explores the rise of feminist neopagan traditions such as Dianic Wicca or Dianic Witchcraft. Named after the Roman goddess Diana, this tradition centers women's experiences and empowerment and all-female covens. It is a departure from traditional Wicca in which men and women worship the male Horned God along with a triple or mother goddess. The late Adler herself was a Wiccan high priestess and a Unitarian Universalist who viewed "paganism as the spiritual side of feminism" and monotheism as "imperialism in religion."[39] Through her writing, she attracted countless feminists to the neopagan movement.

hooks did not publicly identify as a neopagan, but her writing suggests that she, too, was influenced by both that movement and, possibly, spiritualism. In the introduction to *Appalachian Elegy*, her 2012 book of poems, hooks discusses partaking in a ritual to "commune" with her late mother's spirit in the Kentucky hills. In the Buddhist tradition, she started the ritual by chanting, but then she and a group of ecofeminist friends "called forth the ancestors," "spread sage," "planted trees and dug holes for blossoming rose bushes in the name of our mother Rosa Bell."[40]

hooks and her ecofeminist friends operate very much like a coven, an argument strengthened by a poem in *Appalachian Elegy* that honors the witch, the woman with the "wilderness within." In the poem, the "wild woman" is an "aging crone, wise hag" who not only "holds mystery" but can "stir the cauldron," "tend the flames," and "carry messages from the future."[41] This crone sounds very much like hooks' maternal grandmother, Saru, a woman more comfortable outdoors than indoors and who prophesied by interpreting dreams. But the poem may also be an ode to the witch generally, for hooks viewed the Salem witch trials as "an extreme expression of patriarchal society's persecution of women" and a "message to all women that unless they remained within passive, subordinate roles they would be punished, even put to death."[42]

Refusing to be subordinate to men, scores of women became pagans during the second wave feminism movement. But as a women's liberationist who identified primarily as a Buddhist Christian, hooks wanted women involved in widely practiced religions such as Buddhism, Christianity, Judaism, and Islam to feel included in feminism. The problem, she argues in *Feminism Is for Everybody*, wasn't just that the news media ignored the role of spirituality in women's lib but that it emphasized the religious right's criticism of feminists.

Framing feminism as hostile to religion served the purposes of religious fundamentalists who vilified so-called women's libbers. "Indeed, no group has demonized feminists more than right-wing religious fundamentalists who have called for and condoned the murder of feminist thinkers, especially those who support women having reproductive rights," hooks writes.[43] She adds that religious fundamentalism leads people to think that inequality is "natural" and "that control of the female body is necessary."[44] Given this, hooks asserts that feminists need to critique and resist organized patriarchal religion while demonstrating to women of faith that a reimagining of religion is possible:

> When feminist Christians began to offer new and creation-centered critiques and interpretations of the bible, of Christian beliefs, however, women were able to reconcile their feminist politics and sustained commitment to Christian practice. However these activists have yet to fully organize a movement that addresses masses of Christian believers, converting them to an understanding that no conflict need exist between feminism and Christian spirituality. The same is true for those feminists who are Jewish, Buddhist, Muslim, etc. Until that happens organized patriarchal religion will always undermine feminist gains.[45]

But hooks ignores the feminist theology movement that began in the 1960s with the goal of reinterpreting a wide range of religions, including those she lists above, from a feminist perspective. With pioneers such as Valerie Saiving, Rita Gross, Rosemary Radford Ruether, and Fatima Mernissi, the movement challenged the male pronouns typically used to describe God, highlighted the role of women in sacred texts, and advocated for women to serve as clergy members or in other leadership capacities. hooks' omission of feminist theology is curious given that, in *Yearning*, she cites Linell Cady's 1989 essay "Relational Love: A Feminist Christian Vision." It states that love "is a process of integration where the isolation of individuals is overcome through the forging of connections between persons."[46]

Women of color influenced feminist theology with movements specific to their experiences. With leaders such as Jacquelyn Grant, Black women became involved in the womanist theology movement, "recognizing their lives were oppressed in ways not experienced by White women" and finding salvation "in a Jesus they saw as a fully divine, fully human reflection of the pain and suffering they experienced beneath socioeconomic injustice and White supremacy."[47] In a 2004 interview published in an updated edition of *Sisters of the Yam: Black Women and Self-Recovery,* hooks acknowledged the womanist theology movement, pointing out that it has grown immensely since the dawn of second-wave feminism, and that it has "become a place where Christian black women can grow spiritually."[48] She named Katie Cannon, Renita Weems, and Anne Kelly as women whose writings "have offered us new ways to think about black women and feminist theology."[49]

In the mujerista theology movement pioneered by Ada María Isasi-Díaz, Hispanic women celebrate a God who "revindicates the divine image and likeness of women." In the essay "Mujeristas: A Name of Our Own!!," Isasi-Díaz explains that "the mujerista is called to gestate new women and men: a strong people. Mujeristas are anointed by God as servants, prophets and witnesses of redemption. Mujeristas will echo God's reconciling love; their song will be a two-edged sword, and they will proclaim the gospel of liberation."[50]

While these theology movements did not become mainstream trends, the fact that they did occur should not be dismissed. To do so ignores the earnest efforts of feminist believers to reinterpret the patriarchal religions that had long placed them on the periphery.

In the 2022 podcast interview in which she reflected on second-wave feminist spirituality, Starhawk noted that "some women were sort of staying within the established church or within Judaism and the synagogue and trying to open that up and make it more feminist."[51] Starhawk herself strongly considered becoming a rabbi only to rethink the idea after some deliberation. "I thought if I was a rabbi, I'd have to spend a lot of time in services," she said. "But as a witch, I'd have to spend a lot of time dancing naked around the bonfire in the moonlight."[52]

For her, there was no contest between the two.

During the second-wave feminist movement, women reimagined both mainstream and alternative religions to center women's experiences and the divine feminine. But their efforts could not compete with patriarchal religion, the figureheads of which successfully used the mass media as a mouthpiece, hooks laments in *Feminism Is for Everybody.* Unaware of the alternative forms of spirituality available to them, many women remained in patriarchal religious environments due to the mistaken belief that they were the only places where anyone cared about their spiritual lives. By doing so, hooks contends, they missed the opportunity to question outdated belief systems, depict God in diverse ways, respect the sacred feminine, and affirm the importance of spiritual life.

The twenty-first century marked a shift, however. Ushering in both social media and contemporary feminism, the new millennium gave women more opportunities to experiment with religion. Thanks to the internet, those interested in exploring feminist spirituality could do so rather easily, all while making connections with like-minded individuals. By the 2020s, practitioners of feminist spirituality garnered considerable attention from the mainstream news media and attracted large followings on and offline. Simply put, they became some of the nation's best known influencers.

CHAPTER FIVE

Faith without Capitalism and Fundamentalism

Feminism Is for Everybody debuted just a few years before the advent of social media. These networking sites have allowed followers of alternative religions to link up with each other and people curious about such belief systems. Astrologers, tarot card readers, witches, hoodoo practitioners, and Vodou priestesses, many of whom are women or LGTBQ+, are among the individuals who have racked up tens of thousands of followers on Instagram and TikTok.[1]

The trend follows a gradual move away from organized religion in the twenty-first century, with an increasing number of Americans likely to identify as spiritual but not religious, especially young people. According to the Pew Research Center, about 30 percent of Americans identified as having no religion in 2020, a trend projected to result in Christians making up less than half of the US population by 2070.[2]

FEMINIST SPIRITUALITY IN THE TWENTY-FIRST CENTURY

hooks thought it was important for feminists to engage Christianity, in part, because most of the country identified as Christian. But she did not predict while writing *Feminism Is for Everybody* that the new millennium would usher in a generation more interested in neopagan and New Age religions than the Judeo-Christian tradition. hooks could be nearly as critical of New Age spirituality as she was of fundamentalist religions, even as she admired New Age writers such as Marianne Williamson and Wayne Dyer. She also urged Black women to consider New Age concepts instead of limiting their understanding of spirituality to the Black church exclusively.

Still, hooks likely would have questioned the rise of New Age and pagan influencers on social media had she been active on these platforms; she did not use them or the internet generally. She made it clear, though, that she was drawn to spirituality with a focus on social action. "Identifying liberation from any form of domination and oppression as essentially a spiritual quest returns us to a spirituality which unites spiritual practice with their struggles for justice and liberation," she writes in her feminist primer.[3] In contrast, many social media spiritual influencers have been highly capitalistic, addressing social injustice inconsistently or inauthentically.

No shortage of spiritual influencers on social media comes from marginalized groups. Indeed, many fled organized religion because they could not reconcile the messages they heard in institutional places of worship with their gender, sexual orientation, or race. But the marginalization they experienced in organized religion did not necessarily motivate them to tie their spiritual practices to a liberation movement. In fact, these individuals increasingly use social media to profit from services like reading tarot cards or astrology charts. Landing them event gigs, television appearances, and money from promoting a wide range of goods, their spirituality has become their livelihood.

Historically, women healers were community resources. They used their herbal knowledge, sixth sense, prophetic dreams, healing hands, and other spiritual gifts to aid people in their families and communities. In *The Bluest Eye*, the novel hooks credits with changing her life, Morrison shows how indispensable these women were to their communities. But the book also reveals the relational context in which these women healed. They cared about their communities and their communities cared about them, as audiences can see in cinematic depictions of such women in films including 1997's *Eve's Bayou* and 2000's *The Gift*. The transmission of their knowledge involved far more than a financial transaction between strangers.

Online, however, the opposite is true. Earning money through readings, followers accrued, and sponsored content appears to be the primary goal of social media "healers." Fostering relationships with people seeking guidance is secondary, if not irrelevant, to the exchange of cash. There is no shared community between healer and client, and clients looking for a spiritual community must pay to participate. The anticapitalist hooks would not have viewed the meeting of alternative religion and the online marketplace as a positive development. Offline, retailers such as Sephora, Walmart, and Urban Outfitters tried to cash in on the renewed popularity of neopaganism, hawking "witchkits," sage, and healing crystals to consumers.[4]

The capitalist thread running through twenty-first-century feminist spirituality isn't the only cause for concern. Margot Adler points out in the 2006 edition of *Drawing Down the Moon* that many of the young women embracing this spirituality don't know how second wave feminism influenced it:

> Today, a new generation of women is redefining feminist spirituality. Many of them have no real knowledge of the past, but they are also not overwhelmed with the same forms of oppression that burdened feminists in the 1970s. They may come up with different ideas and different forms of organization as a result. Many women have rejected the essentialist thinking that informed much of early spiritual feminism; they simply believe in equal rights for all; they believe that, as Lisa Jervis writes in an essay in LiP magazine: "The actual workings of power will not change with more chromosomal diversity among the powerful."[5]

hooks herself agreed that simply installing women in positions of power would perpetuate patriarchy. Ending domination required the dismantling of systemic oppression, not replacing powerful men with powerful women. That said, redefining feminist spirituality in a way that divorces it from social action would have concerned her. Drawn to neopaganism largely due to films and television shows such as *The Craft, Charmed, Harry Potter,* and *American Horror Story: Coven,* the newest generation of women practicing feminist spirituality likely never viewed these traditions as political. And to some, feminism was less of a political movement than an effort to fight broadly for body positivity, sex positivity, or being a "girlboss," or lean-in corporate feminist. hooks considered lean-in feminism—which takes its name from tech executive Sheryl Sandberg's 2013 book *Lean In: Women, Work, and the Will to Lead*—to be "faux feminism."[6]

In a 2013 essay, hooks writes that the book *Lean In* often comes across as "benevolent patriarchal imperialism,"[7] for Sandberg defines feminism in a way that offers no critique of the current social system. According to hooks, the businesswoman wants women to "run the world," a nod to Beyoncé's 2011 single "Run the World (Girls)" but is unconcerned with changing the world's oppressive structures. "And she makes it seem that privileged white men will eagerly choose to extend the benefits of corporate capitalism to white women who have the courage to 'lean in,'" hooks writes. "It almost seems as if Sandberg sees women's lack of perseverance as more the problem than systemic inequality."[8]

Sandberg's lean-in philosophy also falls short because it assumes that once a critical mass of women occupy corporate leadership roles, traditionally patriarchal work environments will somehow become women friendly. hooks states that women "leaning in" until they reach the top of the corporate ladder won't automatically result in gender equality because "patriarchy has no gender."[9] If systems of domination are not dismantled, women executives will simply perpetuate the same practices as the men they've succeeded. In *Feminism Is for Everybody,* she states,

> While we are told again and again by individual feminist thinkers . . . that women are more caring, more ethical, the facts of how women conduct themselves in relation to less powerful women suggest otherwise. The ethics of care women show in the ethnic or racial groups with which they identify do not extend to those with whom they do not feel empathy, identification, or solidarity. Women of privilege (most

of whom are white but not all) have rapidly invested in the sustained subordination of working-class and poor women.[10]

The following year hooks said that for the first time she felt ambivalent about feminism.[11] She still believed in its tenets but had misgivings about women, be it Sandberg or Hillary Clinton, who had come to represent it in popular culture. She called it "a chaotic moment for feminism globally" due to the many tensions that existed "between feminism and nationalism, feminism and racism."[12] She could not back Clinton, whom she deemed a warhawk, or Sandberg, whom she criticized for being "supportive of various instrumentalities of patriarchy."[13] In the second decade of the twenty-first century, hooks suggested, it had become harder for feminists to distinguish between their allies and their adversaries. One seemed to bleed into the other.

The feminism of the early 2010s was far from radical, but that began to change after Donald Trump's election to president in 2016. Trump had a history of calling women insults such as "fat pigs, dogs, slobs, and disgusting animals."[14] He had been recorded bragging about grabbing women by their genitals and faced allegations of sexual assault and harassment dating back to the 1970s.[15] That such a man defeated Hillary Clinton infuriated women voters from a variety of ethnic, class, and religious backgrounds, including feminist spiritual traditions. Clinton would have been the nation's first woman president and one of the most qualified politicians to fill the role.

Millions of Americans took part in the Women's March on January 21, 2017, to protest Trump's inauguration. Trump's "fiercely anti-woman" viewpoints, the supporters he'd amassed, and the misogyny directed at Clinton disturbed hooks deeply.[16] She admitted during a 2017 appearance at St. Norbert College that she and fellow feminists felt blindsided by the vitriol the election unleashed:

> There were like a ton of anti-Hillary bumper stickers in Kentucky calling her a bitch, saying "lock her up." . . . There was a heartbreak for me because I . . . spent my whole life trying to teach and educate people about the evils of patriarchy. I never imagined that I would live to see a time where patriarchy would become a banner of a leader

of our country, a way to think about greatness. We were done with that. I thought we had allowed men finally a place to be whole, to be emotionally present to their lives. And instead, there's this tremendous gender regression going on.[17]

But women, especially those involved in feminist spirituality, challenged this regression. In 2017, an assortment of "resistance witches" made news headlines for casting spells to bind Trump from doing harm. That same year the #MeToo movement, first launched on MySpace by sexual assault survivor Tarana Burke in 2006, gained national recognition. It inspired sexual misconduct survivors to share their experiences, hold abusers accountable, and fight for more protections for women and vulnerable individuals across industries. Still, many of the individuals who garnered media attention for coming forward as sexual assault survivors were wealthy celebrities. Farmworkers, housekeepers, restaurant servers, and other working-class people who had endured sexual misconduct existed largely in the shadows of the movement, which coincided with Trump's 2018 nomination of Brett Kavanaugh to the US Supreme Court. He was confirmed despite multiple rape allegations. During the confirmation process, witches again made headlines for announcing plans to "hex" Kavanaugh, "all rapists and the patriarchy" at a public gathering.[18]

Event organizer Dakota Bracciale told *Time* magazine that the ritual would serve as an act of resistance and provide a space for sexual assault survivors who refuse to be silent. "We're raising visibility and letting people know they're not alone with the monsters," Bracciale said. "Even the witches are coming out of the woodwork to stop this."[19]

The public hexing ritual harkened back to the late 1960s activism of the group W.I.T.C.H., an acronym that originally stood for Women's International Terrorist Conspiracy from Hell. W.I.T.C.H. used public stunts to challenge patriarchy and capitalism and also supported causes such as the antiwar and student movements. Made up of socialist women, W.I.T.C.H was a secular group but is a notable forerunner to the 1970s feminists who turned to neopaganism to protest patriarchy and empower women.

In the 2010s, the Trump administration was credited with "spawning a new generation of witches."[20] The period during and just after his time in office saw the release of books such as 2017's *Witches, Sluts, Feminists: Conjuring the Sex Positive*, 2019's *Revolutionary Witchcraft*, 2021's *Missing Witches: Recovering True Histories of Feminist Magic*, and 2022's *Hoodoo for Everyone: Modern Approaches to Magic, Conjure, Rootwork, and Liberation*.

Feminist witches again took action when the Supreme Court overturned the landmark *Roe v. Wade* decision in 2022, leaving abortion access up to individual states. They shared reproductive justice spells, abortion access funds, and potential herbal remedies. "The current rash of anti-LGBTQ+ legislation, overtly racist rhetoric and violence and, of course, the dismantling of *Roe v. Wade*, have boosted the attractiveness of magic among women, people of color and other marginalized individuals," Religion News Service noted in June 2022.[21]

Among those drawn to magic during and immediately after the Trump years were women who left the church because they found "its attitude toward sexuality and social issues regressive."[22] While hooks did not abandon the church, she, too, yearned for Christianity with a progressive, nonsexist vision. The church had been a place of refuge for her during her coming of age, but in several works she outlines her concerns with what she labels "fundamentalist Christianity" and describes her connection to practices that stem from African American spirituality rather than organized religion.

CRITIQUING AND RESISTING
REGRESSIVE RELIGION

Growing up in what she characterizes in *Homegrown* as a "Christian patriarchal context" prompted hooks to become a feminist in the first place.[23] She argues that fundamentalist religion is an agent to domesticate, colonize, and subordinate and that racist patriarchal interpretations of Christianity are dangerous influences on people of color. In a worrisome development, she notes, considerable numbers of Black and Hispanic Americans have joined evangelical churches and parrot the heterosexist, militaristic, and fascistic ideologies of church leaders. Given her childhood in a fundamentalist environment, she knew intimately the damage that a church's sexist attitudes could have on the psyche. She recalls,

> My earliest childhood experiences were shaped by fundamentalist Christian beliefs. As much as anything else, they frame what girls could or could not do. For instance, on Sunday girls couldn't wear pants, we couldn't play music, and we couldn't walk across the pulpit. The pulpit was considered a sacred space that a female—of any age—could not walk across, because she would defile it. In church between Sunday school and the morning service, I'd see all the boys running around and crossing the pulpit, but girls were always stopped. It was an early indoctrination into sexist thinking.[24]

In her childhood church, sexism intersected with classism and racism. hooks describes how her mother, Rosa Bell Watkins, distanced herself from the Pentecostal tent meetings that working class and poor people frequented to go to a church that discouraged displays of emotion. This meant that congregants didn't "shout" unless it was the first Sunday of the month, when they could testify and embrace the old ways. A chasm developed between African Americans of Watkins's generation and those of their parents, hooks states. The former began to view shouting as "unseemly."[25]

Although her childhood church was a traditional Black church, race was also an issue there. During her 2014 New School discussion with Gloria Steinem, hooks relayed that her brother struggled to remain a Christian in adulthood because he could not envision Jesus as anything other than a white man. Their church displayed a huge portrait of Jesus painted white, a sight that she and her siblings absorbed throughout their childhood. hooks recalled that the painting included a globe in front of a Jesus with outstretched hands. At the foot of this world appeared people of color. That image still unsettled her brother well into his fifties, demonstrating the importance of representation in the religious realm.

Aware of the harmful impact that Eurocentric depictions of Jesus have had on believers of color, the Catholic Church in 2023 released artwork of Mary and Jesus as Black, Asian, and Middle Eastern. Father Mark Odion of the Catholic Bishops' Conference of England and Wales told British newspaper *The Independent*, "Depictions of the Holy Family have often reflected the culture in which they were created. It is important that we recognise the rich diversity of the Catholic community, not only in England and Wales, but throughout the world."[26] Predictably, the move sparked criticism, mostly from individuals unaware that Mary and Jesus have been portrayed as people of color since antiquity and that research disputes the idea that the pair would have been blonde, blue-eyed, and fair-skinned, as they are commonly depicted.

Regularly confronting a white Jesus at her Black church contributed to hooks' pursuit of Buddhism as a young woman. She saw Buddha represented "in all colors, sizes, shapes, with all different kinds of expressions on the Buddha face," she said.[27] And she collected an assortment of ethnically diverse deities in statue, figurine, and other forms for her home. Sitting among them "alters something within me in the same way that I think Black people who have only had the opportunity to know white Jesus have something altered within them," she said.[28] Seeing a museum exhibit on "Female Buddhas" at the Rubin Museum of Art in New York also had a profound impact on hooks. The exhibit explored Tibetan Buddhism's celebration of the sacred feminine with paintings featuring female teachers, deities, and goddesses known for their capacity to heal. Among these figures are Tara, or "the female Buddha."

Much like the Virgin Mary, Tara is a revered maternal figure with a reputation for protecting her followers from harm. "Tara was once just like us, a mere mortal serving Buddha," according to art critic Benjamin Genocchio. "But once she achieved enlightenment, she took two vows, the first, rather conventionally, to work for all beings until we are enlightened, and the second, rather more radically, to defy tradition of assuming some male form after being reincarnated and to serve others in female form."[29] The Tara art at the exhibit depicted her in a range of hues.

The "incredible" display, according to hooks, had important implications for people of color. "I think that Black people, will we ever really be able to decolonize our minds if we cannot find a way to imagine deities that resemble ourselves?" she asked.[30]

Rather than improve African Americans' self-image, the traditional Black church has played a "conservatizing and colonizing" role in their lives, she asserts in *Homegrown*."[31] But in the book, a multifaceted dialogue between her and Amalia Mesa-Bains—a Mexican-American artist, critic, and scholar—hooks details how Black people have resisted organized religion as well.

When hooks' family engaged nature, erected yard shrines, and used altars in their homes, they challenged institutional Christianity and tapped into the spirituality of their roots. She recalls delighting in the vivid colors—tomato reds and delphinium blues—of the vegetables and flowers her grandmother grew. "This is where I gained a sense of nature as a place where one is grounded and renewed spiritually, and where I learned to value the environment, and understand that I was defined—in part—by my relationship to the earth."[32]

Like the neopagan feminists that she came of age with during the women's liberation movement, hooks valued the power of nature, and specifically, the power of her family matriarch to use land for sustenance in a world hostile to Black female autonomy. Her grandmother's mastery of gardening was just one reminder during hooks' upbringing in the Jim Crow South that white people weren't all-powerful. They could not make the natural world submit to them, even as they subordinated their fellow human beings.

hooks also found that enslavement may have distanced Black Americans from Africa, but it did not sever their ties to the continent entirely. She describes how in the late nineteenth and early twentieth centuries, Southerners could encounter brightly colored shacks with "incredible gardens" and yard shrines honoring the dead, religious icons, or the earth itself. "Folks would sit on the little porches of shotgun houses and meet and greet, display their creativity, share music and stories, with each act revealing African cultural retentions," hooks states.[33]

During enslavement, shrines often went undetected, as white people did not understand how the individuals they held in bondage arranged mounted rocks and herbs in a way that "constituted an altar, a place of power in the life of the powerless," hooks explains.[34] Shrines and altars helped Black Americans engage traditional African spirituality and resist the oppressors who wanted them to disconnect from their roots. After enslavement, Black Americans continued to create shrines and altars despite disapproval from fundamentalist Christian churches. According to hooks,

> The altar was the place you could bring your burdens, lay them down and be restored. I've written about spaces in the African-American Southern home that are shrines made up of photographs and mementos. As a child, I certainly was awed when I stood before the shrines to our ancestors, these shrines that told our family narratives. In childhood, we would learn about the dead from looking at these walls of photographs.... These shrines communicated psychohistory of a genealogy of the soul and graphically showed how traits, interests, beliefs are passed down. And as with Mexican-American women, shrine making offers a spiritual and creative practice to African Americans that is beyond the confines of patriarchy. Making altars was a way to worship, to be restored, and to show devotion.[35]

Although hooks uses past tense to describe altar making, she acknowledged that altars appear throughout the work of assemblage artist Betye Saar, who first came to prominence during the nascent women's liberation movement. Saar cofounded the Los Angeles art collective Womanspace to highlight the work of female artists. In Saar's 1969 work *Black Girl's Window*, a wooden window frame becomes an altar to honor her late father and reference his home in the afterlife via the portrayal of stars, moon, and sky. With the 1975 piece *Record for Hattie*, Saar memorializes her great-aunt Hattie Parson Keys, who died the previous year. She turns a compartmentalized case into an ancestral altar by filling it with her aunt's baby picture and a broken hand mirror, crucifix pendant, and crescent moon and star.

Referring to Saar and her artist daughter Alison, hooks states that "consciously or unconsciously, their work has been informed by Mexican and African-American iconography and tradition. They draw on memories of yard shrines and altars, as well as the cultural hybridity at the heart of the African-American experience."[36]

In 2021, I met and interviewed Betye Saar for British newspaper the *Guardian*.[37] She told me that she'd traveled to various countries in the African diaspora, including Nigeria, Senegal, Haiti, and Brazil. Wherever she traveled, she asked for details about the alternative religions practiced because of her longtime interest in magic and mysticism. By creating mystical art that honors her late elders, Saar worked through trauma about their deaths and other incidents. When she created *Black Girl's Window*, for instance, she was also grieving over a divorce, the Watts rebellion, and King's assassination. Her altar paid tribute to all this loss and rage.

hooks admired King and Malcolm X because both men were prepared to die for their beliefs, to give their lives on "the altar of sacrifice."[38] In this way, the men resemble the "Buddhist nun who self-immolates in sadness and joy, who says, 'I want so badly to let the world know about the meaning of peace that I burn myself; I give myself over,'" hooks says in *Homegrown*.[39] Without this philosophy, building resistance and gaining redemption isn't possible, she adds. A grounding in ancestor worship connects people of color to traditions that honor death and allow them to lead with the "critical vigilance" that's necessary for survival.[40]

Born in 1926, Saar understands the importance of honoring ancestors and engaging magic to manage trauma. Younger Black women, hooks contends in her book *Sisters of the Yam: Black Women and Self-Recovery*, suffer because they're alienated from these traditions. As children, hooks and her siblings thought the homemade salves their Big Mama gave them for ailments had "magical healing powers" but as an adult, hooks realized "that the magic, that power to heal, resided in [Big Mama's] warm, loving, brown hands."[41]

Growing up in Kentucky in the 1950s and '60s, hooks observed elders like Big Mama, who were deeply engaged with "the mystical dimensions of Christian faith."[42] Using the wisdom of both Africans and Native Americans, Black Americans understood "how to be one with the universe and sustain life," hooks writes.[43] Familiar with Black American folk magic, they knew how to heal. Among the healers was hooks' paternal great aunt Sister Ray, a rootworker. "I remember most that people feared her—that she was seen as a woman of power."[44] She intimates that the community viewed Sister Ray as a "witch," the archetype that the women's liberationists embraced to assert their strength as women.

For Black women, the Sister Rays of the community were particularly inspirational. These women gave them pride in their race and their gender, for a Black woman with innate spiritual gifts possessed the tools to oppose domination. As hooks explains in *Sisters of the Yam*,

> In the traditional world of Black folk experience, there was . . . a profound unshaken belief in the spiritual power of black people to transform our world and live with integrity and oneness despite oppressive social realities. In that world, black folks collectively believed in "higher powers," knew that forces stronger than the will and intellect of humankind shaped and determined our existence, the way we lived. And for that reason these black people learned and shared the secrets of healing. They knew how to live well and long despite adversity (the evils caused by racism, sexism, and class exploitation), pain, hardship, unrelenting poverty, and the ongoing reality of loss.[45]

When these individuals used their powers to the fullest, they exuded joy. Moreover, there was no gender division when it came to "magical healing powers."[46] Black women, hooks states, could flex their metaphysical muscles with the same force as their male counterparts. Given this, hooks was shocked when she taught Black students at a prestigious university who lacked knowledge of the old ways, who had no idea how to harness their spiritual power. The new generation, she thought, seemed modern and sophisticated but also spiritually lost.

To help her readers gain spiritual insight, hooks encourages them to spend time in solitude and prayer to gain a "sense of direction."[47] Dreams, she suggests, can provide discernment. She urges readers to connect with the dream interpretation tradition that Black women have taken part in for generations. Keeping a dream book, she states, can empower Black women and improve their understanding of themselves.

While hooks advises Black women to distance themselves from religious fundamentalism and instead advocate for religious practices that are part of "a holistic, progressive beacon of self recovery,"[48] she does not tell readers to step away from organized religion. In a 2004 interview published in *Sisters of the Yam*, hooks said that she blends Christianity and Buddhism and appreciates the latter's "crucial emphasis on mindfulness and daily life."[49] She also cited the Dalai Lama's book *Ethics for a New Millennium* in which he asserts that people can do without organized religion, but they can't do without spirituality.

In *Sisters of the Yam*, hooks argues that spirituality is absent from many Black women's lives because they have been taught to devote themselves to work or family and ignore their personal needs. But Black women's healing depends on them approaching their spirituality in life-sustaining ways. In the interview, hooks expressed her desire for the Black community to have more discussions about New Age spirituality and New Age ways of thinking about the Bible or life generally. While some Black women practice Buddhism, others embrace African-derived religions such as Santería that link them to "the diasporic sense of black woman's selfhood."[50] Whether Black women take up the old ways of their ancestors, combine two spiritual traditions together, or remain in an organized religion, hooks wanted them to have access to the modality most conducive to their healing and spiritual growth. As she put it in 2004,

> Black women deserve to have multiple paths of healing, multiple ways of thinking about spirituality, multiple paths toward recovery. The way is one, and the paths are many. We all need to go somewhere to restore

our souls. We need to be on that path to recovery and to wholeness. Healing body, mind, and spirit redeems us, no matter where we are in our life—lost or found. When we choose to heal, when we choose to love, we are choosing liberation. This is where all authentic activism begins.[51]

For centuries, women have singled out spiritual practices that honor the sacred feminine. Julian of Norwich thought of her savior as a mother, as a woman. First and second-wave feminists popularized spiritualism and neopaganism, respectively. Christian women from diverse ethnic backgrounds launched the feminist, womanist, and mujerista theology movements. And Black American women have used their spiritual gifts to heal loved ones, interpret dreams, work the roots, and honor their ancestors.

A product of the women's liberation movement that promoted feminist spirituality, hooks wanted women to know they had options other than religious fundamentalism. They did not have to worship in institutions that ignored their innate gifts or marginalized them because of their race, class, gender, or sexuality. Rather, hooks hoped that women would engage in spiritual practices that made them feel loved and affirmed. Without such a practice, self-love is not possible, and without self-love, women and men cannot be the partners, parents, or friends they are meant to be.

CHAPTER SIX

"Love Is Everything"

"Shallow, sentimental idealism."[1]

That's how Elise Harris, then a contributing writer to the *New York Times*, sums up her January 30, 2000, review of bell hooks' *All About Love: New Visions*. Borrowing M. Scott Peck's definition, the book describes love as an action that nurtures one's own or another person's spiritual growth. Since society teaches that love is a feeling devoid of spirituality, lovelessness is pervasive, hooks contends. Most people have never known true love—be it in romantic, familial, or friendship contexts—and they won't until they view love through a spiritual lens, she argues.

Drawing on Buddhist, Protestant, Catholic, and New Age traditions as well as humanistic psychology, hooks grounds love in religion. Her radical politics also inform her characterization of love, for she states that the antidotes to lovelessness include emotional honesty and commitment, the liberation of children, the end of gender essentialism, and rejection of patriarchal and capitalist norms. Considering how hooks complicates the discussion of love to make space for spirituality and politics, it is unclear how *All About Love* reads as shallow or sentimental. By urging readers to shift how they view love—from a feeling to an action, from chemistry to spirituality, from the personal to the political—it is one of hooks' most provocative books.

To be clear, Harris's review does not totally excoriate *All About Love*. In fact, she applauds hooks for asserting that love between friends or community members is as important as love between close relatives or romantic partners. Harris also compliments hooks for arguing that love takes labor and that "work and money have replaced the values of love and community, and this must be reversed."[2]

Overall, however, the review is dismissive of *All About Love* and of hooks. Essentially reducing the book to "pop sociology," Harris accuses hooks of using past partnerships to generalize about how men and women approach romantic partnerships. She suggests that the feminist fails to consider that not all relationships fall victim to sexist gender constructs. But hooks never states that all romantic partnerships play out in this way; she simply infers that this problem is extremely common and cites not just her own experiences to make this point but popular dating books such as *The Rules* and *Men Are from Mars, Women Are from Venus* that reinforce sexism by framing men and women as inherently different from each other. Years after hooks wrote *All About Love*, dating books debuted that continued to characterize men and women as if they're from two different planets. Among those books are the bestsellers *Act Like a Lady, Think Like a Man* and *He's Just Not That into You*, both of which were made into major motion pictures that exposed an even wider audience to the gender essentialist views of their male authors.

In her review, Harris acknowledges that partners in both heterosexual and homosexual relationships tend to adhere to fixed gender roles, but she argues that hooks does not go into sufficient detail about the source of this behavior. In doing so, Harris ignores that *All About Love* is not a treatise on gender roles but an exploration of love across a broad range of relationship types. She also overlooks the book's many passages that explain how patriarchy results in people using lies and manipulation to vie for power in relationships. Women and men just employ different methods, the ones most socially acceptable for their gender, to gain control. The widespread idea that men and women have innately distinct desires in love and relationships perpetuates gender norms, too. Ultimately, hooks concludes, patriarchy leads to unfulfillment, disconnection, and even "intimate terrorism"[3] in romantic partnerships, friendships, and family relationships.

Throughout her critique, Harris uses veiled misogyny to attack hooks. She indirectly compares hooks to both Pollyanna, the blindly optimistic children's book protagonist, and Sleeping Beauty, the fairy tale princess. The reviewer particularly opposes *All About Love*'s engagement of spirituality, including a passage on angels, to frame the book as "clichéd" and "emotional."[4] What Harris leaves out is that hooks discusses the cultural fixation on angels to segue into an analysis of the biblical hero Jacob, whose struggles don't end once he meets his soulmate, Rachel.

Devoting several pages to Jacob, hooks writes a sermon of sorts on the significance of his spiritual journey after love enters his life. Jacob's story is a reminder that love "provides us with the means to cope with our difficulties and ways that enhance our growth," hooks asserts. "Having worked and waited for love, Jacob becomes psychologically strong. He calls upon that strength when he must once again enter the wilderness to journey home."[5] When Jacob wrestles with an angel, the encounter teaches him that "there is joy in struggle," for "the blessing the angel gives to Jacob comes in the form of the wound."[6] hooks does not discuss angels in the airy-fairy way that Harris insinuates, but to underscore that love and difficulty often intersect.

Harris states that once "the philosophy of love was a fine sub-ject for the man of ideas, like Erich Fromm or C. S. Lewis,"[7] but apparently not so for hooks. Men quoted in the book, such as the Rev. Martin Luther King Jr. and Thomas Merton, would have never started a paragraph discussing their mothers, as hooks does, Har-ris posits. Though King and Merton are "master rhetoricians," she writes, hooks' "best points are simple ones."[8] It's telling that Harris never mentions the women, such as Sharon Salzberg, Harriet Lerner, Marianne Williamson, and Teresa of Ávila, referenced in the book, as if only men's ideas about the topic matter. All the while, the *Times* disregards that hooks did not capitalize her name, a fact that was well known when *All About Love* debuted.

The unfavorable review did not dampen interest in *All About Love*. The book remains one of hooks' most popular and has been name-checked by an eclectic mix of public figures including model and actress Emily Ratajkowski; filmmaker Sofia Coppola; poet Lee Herrick; professor, lecturer, and author Brené Brown; and novelist Emily St. John Mandel, who told Slate, "That book changed how I think about friendship."[9]

ALL ABOUT LOVE'S ENDURING POPULARITY

While *All About Love* is not flawless, it distinguishes itself from other books on the topic by focusing on a variety of relationships, exploring how patriarchy is the opposite of loving, and discussing love from a political and spiritual perspective rather than a romantic one. Moreover, hooks practices what she preaches. She opens up about her own relationships just as she encourages readers to open up if they want true love.

For these reasons, *All About Love* has had a remarkably long shelf life. In the early 2020s, the book enjoyed renewed interest as COVID-19 spread across the globe, prompting the public to reevaluate their lives and relationships. When hooks died in late 2021, Rachel Kahan, her editor at William Morrow, discussed the continued fascination with the feminist's work. Noting *All About Love*'s debut on the *New York Times* bestseller list during the pandemic, Kahan told Oprah Daily,

> What gives me the greatest joy about bell hooks' work is that it's being eagerly embraced by so many new readers right now in our current cultural moment, not only in the U.S. but around the world. When *All About Love* hit the *New York Times* bestseller list last year for the very first time, two decades after it was first published, bell and I shared an incredibly emotional moment on the phone, laughing—almost giddy. We were both so thrilled to see that the fruits of her labor kept multiplying from generation to generation.[10]

During the COVID-19 lockdowns of 2020, when families spent more time together as many jobs and schools went remote and options for entertainment outside the home were limited, it's not surprising that interest in *All About Love* spiked. News reports during the first phases of the pandemic provided a grim outlook for domestic life. Headlines focused on marriages falling apart, young people's mental health declining, and mothers crumbling as they tried to balance remote work with their children's distance learning. With youth feeling unsupported by their parents and wives feeling unsupported by their husbands, patriarchy during the onset of the pandemic affected families as *All About Love* suggests it would have—many fathers shirking their caretaking responsibilities and many children powerless in homes where parents, particularly mothers, resented them.

Already considered more important than friendships in society, family relationships were centered intensely as pandemic lockdowns confined people to their homes. This left untold numbers of single people cut off from their support networks. Far from anomalous, single-person households make up a significant percentage of US households. In 1960, such households only constituted 13 percent of the nation's households, but that figure more than doubled to 29 percent in 2022, according to the US Census Bureau.[11] Americans aged fifty and up are even more likely to reside alone, with women making up 60 percent of older people living by themselves.[12] hooks discussed the trend of women living independently during a 2017 appearance at St. Norbert College:

I always tell people that the feminist backlash isn't happening because feminism was such a failure. It was because feminism was such a powerful movement. If you're following all the sort of sociological literature that's coming out about Americans living alone, a massive number of those women that are now living alone are women over 40, over 50. And we're being told that it's feminism, not in fact, that it's women fleeing patriarchy. I mean, women who have been in abusive relationships with men or just dominating relationships. [They] aren't like me; they're not trying to find a partner. They say, "Girl, I don't ever want to do that again." My sisters say, "Oh, yeah, you think you want a husband? If you had one, you'd be trying to get rid of him like the rest of us."[13]

Previously, hooks discussed the difficulty of finding anything other than patriarchal mentalities in men her age. This led her to reconsider her quest for male companionship. Having turned her home into a loving environment filled with literature, art, and photography that nurtured her, she didn't want to risk inviting a man into her home, only for him to sow discord in her sacred space.

Unlike earlier generations of women, many twenty-first-century women do not have to enter or remain in unfulfilling marriages for economic survival. Living alone, women are prioritizing their health and wellness, exploring their personal interests, and forming connections with people outside the institution of marriage. Research indicates that single women without children are happier than their married and parenting counterparts.[14]

"Knowing how to be solitary is central to the art of loving," hooks writes in *All About Love*. "When we can be alone, we can be with others without using them as a means of escape."[15] As fewer women partner with troubled men to avoid being alone, psychologists are warning about an uptick of lonely men, a trend they predict will worsen. Men make up nearly two-thirds of dating app users, according to a 2022 *Psychology Today* article that advised men to improve their communication skills and learn how to become emotionally available to increase their chances of finding a mate, as men are usually happier when romantically partnered. The article warned, however, that many families do not consistently teach boys how to emotionally connect, a critical skill since it is "the lifeblood of healthy, long-term love."[16]

Some single people—especially women who would otherwise be in unfulfilling relationships—are perfectly content, but aging may complicate matters. Individuals growing old in single-person households may be more likely to develop mental and physical health problems and more likely to be lonely than their peers living with others. Nearly seventy when she died, hooks was among the nation's elderly and single population. She did not keep her desire for a partner a secret and discussed publicly that she had spent more than a decade celibate following her last relationship breakup.[17] hooks had her fears about aloneness, recalled her friend Lynnée Denise, who sent her poetry and tinctures to keep her company during the pandemic. "When we spoke by phone, she talked about not wanting to die alone—and not wanting to be part of a legacy of Black women scholars who die prematurely, get quoted, excavated, rendered a once-was figure in the archive without being fully honored for their complexity," Denise revealed in the *L.A. Times* after hooks died.[18]

Young people may be even more likely to suffer from loneliness than their elderly counterparts. A research study conducted during fall 2020 found that 61 percent of young adults aged eighteen to twenty-five felt lonely during pandemic lockdowns,[19] but youth loneliness was escalating well before the COVID-19 crisis. A 2019 YouGov poll found that 22 percent of millennials reported having no friends, 27 percent reported having "no close friends," 30 percent reported having "no best friends," and 25 percent reported having no acquaintances—all higher percentages than Gen Xers and baby boomers reported about their social connections.[20]

Researchers have found that teens aren't as likely to be sexually active as older generations either.[21] This is a positive development if it means teens are abstinent because they refuse to be pressured into physical intimacy. The trend has also been linked to lower rates of teen pregnancy and sexually transmitted infections. Yet, officials have flagged the decline in teen sex as a possible warning sign that young people aren't connecting with each other in the ways their predecessors did.

Studies indicate that twentysomethings struggle to form romantic connections, too. A Stanford University researcher reported in 2017 that just half of unpartnered heterosexual women in this age group went on a date during the year prior.

Youth loneliness is a phenomenon without a single cause, but experts have pointed to mental illness, financial instability, television binge-watching, online pornography, workaholism, social media, and "hookup" culture as contributing factors. hooks discusses youth loneliness in *All About Love*, her insights into the issue relevant decades after the book's release. "I began to speak more openly about the place of spirituality in my life when witnessing the despair of my students, their sense of hopelessness, their fears that life is without meaning, their profound loneliness and lovelessness," hooks recalls.[22]

Whether they were married or single, young or elderly, Americans faced unique challenges during the pandemic that led them to reflect on their relationships. This explains their attraction to a book such as *All About Love* that aims to teach them how to truly love their families, friends, communities, and themselves. Although news headlines during the pandemic's first year emphasized how lockdowns were harmful to families, research conducted later contradicted such press reports. For example, divorces actually dropped by 12 percent during 2020,[23] the pandemic year when state legislators issued stay-at-home orders to the public. And youth suicides fell during remote learning, only rising again when in-person classes resumed,[24] with US Surgeon General Vivek Murthy issuing an advisory in December 2021 urging school officials, families, and others to take action to support young people in crisis.[25]

By the end of 2022, experts from online dating platforms such as Match were discussing how the pandemic led to nearly three-quarters of single people desiring committed relationships and no longer emphasizing superficial qualities, such as physical appearance, in potential partners.[26] "Instead, 92% of singles now rank 'emotional maturity' and 'comfortably communicating their needs and wants' among the most important traits," Match's twelfth annual Singles in America study found.[27] "And the No. 1 attribute most singles are looking for is someone they can trust and confide in. This bodes well for longer, healthier relationships."[28]

Meanwhile, research from the Kinsey Institute at Indiana University found "that 74% of married couples surveyed in late 2020 felt the pandemic strengthened their marriage, and 82% said it made them feel more committed."[29]

As people prioritized interpersonal connections during the pandemic, in which a combined 835,000 Americans died in 2020 and 2021,[30] they took steps to deemphasize work's hold on their lives. To enable them to continue spending quality time with their loved ones, many employees demanded to keep working remotely after COVID-19 restrictions were lifted. Some remote workers even left overpriced big cities for less populated areas where their families could enjoy a better quality of life. Millions of workers quit their jobs altogether—ushering in a trend that became known as the "Great Resignation." Beyoncé's 2022 hit single "Break My Soul" referenced the cultural changes unfolding during the pandemic. In it, she discusses falling in love, quitting stressful and unrewarding jobs, and searching for a "new foundation" in life.[31]

But it is another song, Jackie Wilson's 1967 classic "Higher and Higher," that hooks felt best captures the type of love discussed in *All About Love.* As she told NPR in 2000,

> What I like about this Jackie Wilson song is that it's a male singer who's singing about how, when he meets this woman, she guides him; she offers him a love that is restorative to his being. . . . To know love, we must surrender our attachment to sexist thinking in whatever form it takes in our lives, and some sexist thinking makes many men feel that they don't have anything to learn from women. So the fact that in this song, Jackie Wilson is talking about how one person can feel like life just has beaten them down and they haven't been able to find that spark out of the depression or the sadness, and then someone ignites that spark, and they can transform their reality, and that's what I like about it. And it's just such an upbeat sense of, you know, don't you just feel, like, lifted up when you hear that music?[32]

As the pandemic inspired the public to "lift up" their relationships and personal lives, *All About Love* appeared on the *New York Times* bestseller list in both 2021 and 2022. The book provides a "new foundation" for people seeking love, one that grounds love in spiritual practice and frames love as a force diametrically opposed to imperialist, white supremacist, capitalist patriarchy. The book stands out not only because it reimagines love but also because it is one of the first works in which hooks discusses her religious faith in depth.

LOVE AND SPIRITUALITY

Before *All About Love* even begins, hooks leaves no doubt that the book has a spiritual focus. On the dedication page, she quotes a passage in the biblical book of Song of Solomon that states, "I found him whom my soul loves. I held him and would not let him go." In this context, hooks explains, love is "to holding on, to knowing again that moment of rapture, of recognition where we can face one another as we really are, stripped of artifice and pretense, naked and not ashamed."[33]

Having a clear definition of love would make it easier for people to love genuinely, hooks argues, but love is too often considered a feeling and not an action. Instead of loving others, people typically "cathect with them," meaning they "invest feelings or emotions" into an individual that has become important to them. But to truly love, people must practice "care, affection, recognition, respect, commitment, and trust as well as honest and open communication."[34] Mistaking cathexis for true love leads even abusive people to insist that they love the person—a child, spouse, friend—they purport to love but harm instead. The recognition that love is "the will to nurture our own and another's spiritual growth" makes it impossible to claim that love and abuse can occur simultaneously.[35] Acknowledging this truth, however, makes people uncomfortable because they would have to admit that their dearest relationships, be they with a romantic partner, parent, or friend, are not loving. Many people feel cared for by others but are not actually loved by them, as real love is not the norm, according to hooks.

Contending that lovelessness is rampant in society, hooks writes that a spiritual awakening can revive a "a culture that is dead to love."[36] Although most Americans identify in some way as spiritual, if not religious, they don't nurture their interest in spiritual life as they should because individualism, capitalism, and power compete for their attention in a society that values the material over the spiritual. But when one leads a life connected to "divine spirit," they see love in every "living being," hooks writes.[37] Leading a life disconnected from divinity, in contrast, results in a pursuit of material goods that ultimately produces spiritual emptiness.

Regularly attending a place of worship does not effectively counteract the forces of materialism and capitalism because the love of money has infiltrated these sacred spaces too. The prosperity gospel—a line of religious thought that suggests faith, positive thinking, or financial devotion to a church will result in believers achieving good fortune—can be traced as far back as 1,600 years ago when St. Augustine lived and discussed his views on wealth.[38] An opponent of the prosperity gospel, he warned against avarice, describing the accumulation of material possessions as "uncleanness of the heart."[39] Despite Augustine's warnings, the prosperity gospel has endured for centuries. In the latter half of the twentieth century, the newest version of this philosophy began to spread and continues to have a hold on Christians, New Agers, and other believers today. In 2006, the documentary and book *The Secret* debuted with the message that the law of attraction could be used to generate wealth and success in life. Tens of millions of the DVD alone sold.

In 2007, Senator Chuck Grassley, a Republican from Iowa, initiated a probe into the finances of pastors associated with prosperity gospel–style preaching. He decided to investigate after receiving complaints about the lavish homes, luxury jets, and expensive cars of these preachers. A National Public Radio article on the investigation mentioned a DVD released by televangelist the Rev. Creflo Dollar called *Does God Want You to Be Poor?*[40] According to the aptly named Dollar, faith can help believers turn poverty into abundance.

More than a decade after the federal government investigated prosperity gospel preachers for alleged financial misconduct, headlines appeared in 2020 about why megachurches closely affiliated with President Donald Trump received the most COVID-19 financial relief from the government.[41] In early 2021, staffers from the global megachurch Hillsong claimed that pastors there used tithe money to buy fancy meals and high-end clothing.[42] That same year marked the debut of the book *PreachersNSneakers: Authenticity in an Age of For-Profit Faith and (Wannabe) Celebrities*, which examines the prevalence of capitalism and conspicuous consumption in churches.

As an anticapitalist scholar, hooks objected to trends such as prosperity theology, arguing in *All About Love* that it can be used to suggest that people who financially struggle do so because they simply lack the will to attract wealth into their lives. Poor people, rather than a stratified economic system that gives a powerful minority control of most wealth, are blamed for poverty. hooks not only criticized the prosperity gospel in Christian denominations but also in Buddhist ones such as Nichiren Shoshu, which attracted a following of African Americans, among them the late singer Tina Turner. The root of income inequality is greed, she writes, asserting that it has rightly been characterized as a "deadly sin" because it results in people disregarding the common good and human connectedness. Of greed, she says,

> It wipes out individual recognition of the needs and concerns of everyone, replacing this awareness with harmful self-centeredness. Healthy narcissism (the self-acceptance, self-worth, that is the cornerstone of self-love) is replaced by a pathological narcissism (wherein only the self matters) that justifies any action that enables the satisfying of desires. The will to sacrifice on behalf of another, always present when there is love, is annihilated by greed. No doubt this explains our nation's willingness to deprive poor citizens of government-funded social services while huge sums of money fuel the ever-growing culture of violent imperialism.[43]

hooks did not just object to greed but also to how fundamentalists from all faiths use doctrine to "justify supporting imperialism, militarism, sexism, racism, homophobia." In doing so, "they deny the unifying message of love that is at the heart of every major religious tradition."[44] During and after Trump's 2016 journey to the presidency, white evangelicals became closely aligned with bigotry in the public consciousness. They overwhelmingly supported the mogul-turned-president known for his remarks and policies targeting migrants, Muslims, women, people of color, and people with disabilities. Despite his hateful comments and harmful actions, such as separating migrant parents and children at the US-Mexico border,

Trump received the backing of white religious voters during his 2016 and 2020 presidential campaigns.[45]

When imperialist white supremacist capitalist patriarchy spreads in the church, it opposes the Scriptures that declare believers are one in Christ, *All About Love* posits. In the book, hooks urges Christians, and all believers, to practice their religions as they were intended to be, to lift up society "by being loving."[46]

As she challenges people of faith to set a better example, hooks also lists ways that religious groups have answered the call to be loving through their contributions to society. She describes Buddhists in the US working to liberate Tibet, Christians providing food and shelter for people in need globally, and liberation theology inspiring the oppressed with a spiritual vision focused on ending domination. "These embodiments of loving practice renew our hope and restore the soul all around the world," she writes.[47]

hooks' idea of what it means for religious groups to be loving echoes the epistle of James, which includes the oft-quoted Scripture that "faith without works is dead."[48] Genuinely loving believers have works to show for it. They fight against political injustice, meet the needs of the poor, and work for the liberation of the oppressed. She counted German psychoanalyst Erich Fromm, King, and Merton—all of whom she cites in *All About Love*—as personal influences because their work frames love as the best force to stop domination.

The trio all have a connection to Buddhism. King had a fateful meeting with Thích Nhất Hạnh that inspired him to publicly oppose the Vietnam War. Born in 1900 to Orthodox Jewish parents, Fromm viewed Buddhism as an exemplary humanistic practice because its "main goal is exactly that of liberating man from all dependence, activating him, showing him that he, and nobody else, bears the responsibility for his fate."[49] He also befriended Zen Buddhist leader D. T. Suzuki, appearing with him at the 1957 Zen Buddhism and Psychoanalysis conference that led to the subsequent book *Zen Buddhism and Psychoanalysis*. Later, Fromm would criticize the commercialization of spirituality, arguing that Buddhist meditation should be used to help people become self-actualized and fight against political and economic injustice.

Like Fromm, Merton also became friendly with Suzuki after exploring Buddhism in the 1950s. The long correspondence between the men appears in *Zen and the Birds of Appetite*, a book by Merton published after his sudden 1968 death during a monastic conference in Thailand. Merton may have been ordained in the Catholic priesthood, but he was strongly drawn to Zen Buddhism, believing the spiritual path was not just compatible with Christianity but similar to it, particularly in its approach to suffering. According to Merton,

> Both Christianity and Buddhism show that suffering remains inexplicable, most of all for the man who attempts to explain it in order to evade it, or who thinks explanation itself is an escape. Suffering is not a "problem" as if it were something we could stand outside of and control. Suffering, as both Christianity and Buddhism see, each in its own way, is part of our very ego-identity and empirical existence, and the only thing to do about it is to plunge right into the middle of contradiction and confusion in order to be transformed by what Zen calls "the great death" and Christianity calls "dying and rising with Christ."[50]

Merton argued that an age of religious maturity had arrived that made it perfectly acceptable for Christians to become students of spiritual practices such as Buddhism and Hinduism. Like King, Merton admired the nonviolent Hinduism of Mahatma Gandhi and advocated for pacifism. Along with Gandhi and Suzuki, Merton's influences included Thích Nhất Hạnh and the Dalai Lama. Most importantly, he had a guiding belief that love mattered more than anything.

M. Scott Peck, author of *The Road Less Traveled*, from which hooks took her definition of love, identified as a Christian but often drew on Buddhist principles in his work. Influenced by Fromm, Peck begins *The Road Less Traveled* by acknowledging that the first of the "Four Noble Truths" Buddha learned was "life is suffering."[51] Echoing Merton, he writes that the way out of suffering is to accept the difficulty of life.

These men offer insight into hooks' spiritual vision. Born into the Judeo-Christian tradition, they found inspiration in Zen Buddhism and were moved to fight for social action, all while championing the importance of love for humanity. hooks regretted that contemporary writing about love typically omits the idea that love is a political act and that the strength to love comes from an engaged spiritual life.

In the church of her youth, hooks first learned that "God is love" and encountered characterizations of love that challenge the pervasive notion that love and abuse can coexist. Her church exposed her to child liberation theology, albeit not by that name but through the idea that children "were special in the heart and mind of divine spirit."[52] The divine spirit is her term for how the "forces that are beyond human desire or will alter circumstances and/or guide and direct us."[53] Some people call these forces by names including "soul, God, the Beloved, higher consciousness, or higher power"[54] and others insist these forces cannot be named at all, a nod to Exodus 3:14, when Moses asks God his name and God answers, "I am who I am."

Although hooks offers several criticisms of religious institutions in *All About Love*, she writes that she found a "a space of redemption" in her childhood church through the belief that "we are all one, that love is all."[55] She asserts that spiritual life, above all else, is about dedication to a line of thought and action that centers interconnectedness. Since love and spirituality are not valued in the academy, hooks states, she turned to the Scriptures in which she read about love as a child to keep her from "hardening [her] heart" as a grad school student.[56] Having valued the mind above everything else as a young person, she learned from the Bible that there is no comparison between a sharp mind and a loving heart. To nurture her spiritual life as a graduate student, hooks revealed in *All About Love* that she repeatedly reflected on these lines from Corinthians:

> If I speak with the tongues of men and of angels, but have not love, I am a noisy gong or a clanging cymbal. And if I have prophetic powers, and understand all mysteries and all knowledge, and if I have all faith so as to remove mountains, but have not love, I am nothing. If I give away all I have, and if I deliver my body to be burned, but have not love, I gain nothing.[57]

To demonstrate how important love is, Scripture states that even rare and powerful spiritual gifts such as speaking in tongues, prophetic abilities, and miraculous faith would mean little without it. A person can make enormous sacrifices—giving away all of one's wealth or one's very life—but these acts would be insignificant minus love. Consulting Corinthians helped hooks put her experience in the academy into perspective: Intellect is not remotely as important as love is.

Her time in graduate school may have been trying, but she cautions her readers against turning to spiritual practice only when life is difficult. Instead, one should engage the spiritual consistently, and in so doing, "recognize divine spirit everywhere."[58] As her maternal grandmother believed, one needn't take part in organized religion to be a spiritual person, hooks writes. By meditating, praying, communing in nature, serving others, or choosing to remain connected to the divine forces "that inform our inner and outer world," people can lead spirit-filled lives.[59]

In her spiritual life, hooks, of course, took cues from Buddhism and Christianity. From the latter, she learned that "anyone who does not know love is still in death,"[60] as 1 John 3:14 states. And from Sharon Salzberg, author and teacher of Buddhist meditation methods, she learned that spiritual practice is "the liberation of the heart which is love."[61]

How individuals express their spirituality is entirely up to them, hooks contends. But fellowshipping with other believers is important no matter one's faith, as it provides inspiration. hooks, for one, meditated, prayed, and attended Buddhist and Christian gatherings. "My belief that God is love—that love is everything, our true destiny—sustains me. I affirm these beliefs . . . through contemplation and service, through worship and loving kindness."[62]

By connecting to divine forces through spiritual practice, feelings of isolation can dissipate and be replaced with optimism. As such, it is crucial for everyone to know what their spirit needs, hooks writes. This understanding is not just important because it can alleviate feelings of hopelessness, but because it leads to spiritual awakening that, in turn, leads to love. No matter the relationship, whether it is with the self or others, love is the key to nurturing spiritual growth.

In the United States, people are conditioned to prioritize one kind of love above all others—romantic love. The stuff of trashy novels, vapid romcoms, bad poetry, and sexist reality TV, the romantic love that society focuses on has little link to any sort of spirituality. As a result, countless people continue to long for the fairy-tale love that has eluded them, unaware that true love requires the fostering of spiritual growth and not just the chemical high that occurs when one "falls in love," a term hooks proposed should be reworded. Reframing romantic love to include a spiritual component makes true love possible.

CHAPTER SEVEN

New Visions of Romance and Relationships

When the rapper Lil' Kim was just twenty-two years old, she dropped her debut album, *Hard Core*. The title references both her hard-hitting rap style and her sexually explicit song lyrics. Released in November 1996, the album would go on to become double platinum and make *Rolling Stone*'s list of best debut albums of all time. Just seven months after Kim (née Kimberly Jones) released the album that would make her a rap legend, she sat down with hooks for an interview in *Paper* magazine.

In the lead up to the Q&A, hooks code switches from her standard academic writing style. She uses profanity and slang to make her writing digestible to a younger audience and to Kim's fanbase in particular. She also subverts the widespread image of Kim as a "ho . . . nothing but a prostitute" to a woman who is "young, pretty and sweet—just plain old-fashioned feminine." She adds, "Lil' Kim has the kind of innocence it's possible to work with and work over." Moreover, hooks characterizes Kim as intellectually savvy, a performer who "knows when it's fantasy and when it's real, when it's about getting paid or getting free."[1]

Kind and compassionate throughout the interview, hooks prompted Kim to discuss sexuality, image, feminism, and greed.

But when hooks asked Kim about love, the rapper responded immediately, "I don't have that." She confessed that she recently ended a relationship with a man who deeply hurt her and that she experienced emotional abuse in numerous relationships. "It seems like everywhere I go I can't get real love," she said, adding that despite boyfriends who disparaged her looks, "I know that I can be beautiful inside." Having a spiritual life helps her, she told hooks.[2]

In *All About Love*, released three years after the *Paper* magazine interview, hooks admits to being flabbergasted by Kim's response to the question about love. How could a woman who managed to accumulate fame and wealth despite a lack of education and an upbringing in a "broken" family believe in herself enough to overcome numerous race, class, and gender barriers but doubt she'd ever know love? In addition, Kim expressed more interest in discussing wealth than in discussing love during the interview. hooks writes,

> The culture of greed validates and legitimizes her worship of money; it is not at all interested in her emotional growth. Who cares if she ever knows love? Sadly, like so many Americans, she believes that the pursuit and attainment of wealth will compensate for all emotional lack. Like so many of our nation's citizens, she does not pay close attention to the mass media messages that tell us about the emotional suffering of the rich. If money really made up for loss and lovelessness the wealthy would be the most blissful people on the planet. Instead, we would do well to remember again the prophetic lyric song by The Beatles: "Money can't buy me love."[3]

But even those desperately searching for romantic love may not be ready to receive it, according to hooks. Society has taught them to believe that "someday our prince will come" or that they will soon meet the "girl of our dreams."[4] After they meet, then what happens? Many people aren't prepared to grow the infatuation stage of a relationship into a more substantial connection, let alone consider how a childhood in which they were abused, neglected, shamed, or otherwise traumatized might affect their adult partnerships. While hooks argues that not all relationship hopefuls are ready to receive love, it's important to consider that those looking for "Mr. or Mrs. Right" may not be ready to give love either.

hooks herself reveals in *All About Love* that she found it difficult to evaluate whether she could give the love she wanted to get. Instead of giving love, individuals all too often yearn to get their needs met, especially those needs that derive from painful childhoods. Depicted in love songs and love stories, this sort of romantic love has more to do with fantasy than with spiritual growth.

LOVE IS NOT A FEELING

The hope of being swept off one's feet is dangerous because it prevents people from pursuing true love, causing them to settle for mere romance. hooks references Morrison's *The Bluest Eye* to support her argument, as the novel posits that romantic love is one "of the most destructive ideas in the history of human thought."[5] That's because this kind of idealized love tends to end in disillusionment. According to hooks, it also suggests that people do not choose to love, that love is not an action but a force that occurs against one's will: if one falls in love, the individual bears no responsibility in the relationship.

Merton criticizes the phrase *fall in love* in his essay "Love and Need." The expression, he argues, "reflects a peculiar attitude toward love and life itself—a mixture of fear, awe, fascination, and confusion. It implies suspicion, doubt, hesitation in the presence of something unavoidable, yet not fully reliable."[6]

Citing Merton's concerns, as well as Fromm's, hooks tells readers that love is not a feeling. What she doesn't address, however, are the biochemical processes that take place when people do fall in love, convincing them that their feelings at the time are indeed significant. Brain imaging of people in love reveals that neurochemicals cause them to feel so smitten that they desire to make their beloved a mate.

When people are in love, scans have found, they're inundated with the neurotransmitter dopamine, which is associated with pleasure. And having sex can cause a person to be overwhelmed with oxytocin, known as the "love hormone" because it leads people to form emotional bonds. Also released is vasopressin, which causes people to feel protective of their partners, thus inducing feelings of attachment in them. This is not a strictly human phenomenon, as more than one hundred species of animals have dopamine systems that cause them to feel romantic love, according to neurosurgeon Dr. Philip Stieg. No matter the species, falling in love can feel like an addiction. Stieg explains,

> The area of the brain that produces dopamine and lights up when we're in love is near other regions that control thirst and hunger. So, it feels all-consuming because it is all-consuming—and it's meant to spur us into action. This biological drive evolved millions of years ago to give us the ability to focus intently on another member of our species and mate.[7]

The euphoric feelings these brain chemicals produce wane after a couple of years. Dopamine, oxytocin, and vasopressin alone do not foster long-term relationships built on trust, communication, and honesty—elements hooks asserts are necessary for real love to occur. Once these feelings wear off, people can better determine if they have found the right mate. Unfortunately, some individuals make major commitments, such as getting married, having children, or buying property, with someone during the "madly in love" stage of a relationship. They risk committing to partners with whom they have little in common, with whom they experience lovelessness in the end.

Addicted to the passion present in the beginning of a courtship, other people abandon partners once a relationship seemingly turns stale. Chasing the thrill of new love, they replace old partners with new prospects, only to repeat the cycle. These individuals will never know true love, according to neurologist Dr. Fred Nour, author of *True Love: How to Use Science to Understand Love*. Everyone experiences the stage of falling out of love with a partner, Nour told *The Today Show*. "In a culture that focuses almost solely on romantic love, it can be very alarming when you realize the rush is gone, the passion has vanished, and your spouse no longer makes your pulse race," he said.[8] But sticking around when the passion dries up provides the opportunity for people to experience true love, a gradual process that creates a deep bond between a couple eventually.

To normalize a definition of love that goes beyond "falling in love," hooks suggests in *All About Love* that people drop the phrase, though in a way that doesn't prevent them from discussing when they feel a spark with someone. She recommends that people say, "I've connected with someone in a way that makes me think I'm on the way to knowing love" instead of "I think I'm in love." Alternatively, one might say "I am loving" or "I will love" instead of "I am in love." These changes have the potential to get people to recognize love as a lasting and spiritual force rather than a passing feeling. "Our patterns around romantic love are unlikely to change if we do not change our language," hooks states.[9]

Changing the wording used to describe love paves the path for people to experience relationships rooted in care, respect, intention, will, and responsibility. This is the love that satisfies, hooks contends, not the love hormones that dissipate and leave disillusionment in their stead. In addition to the term *falling in love*, hooks takes issue with New Age spirituality's take on love, arguing that it makes it seem like "everything will always be wonderful if we are just loving."[10] In reality, people will still experience conflicts, betrayals, and other problems despite how loving they are. According to hooks, love simply enables one "to confront these negative realities in a manner that is life-affirming and life-enhancing."[11] Such was the case with the Bible's Jacob after he met Rachel.

Some New Age discussions about soulmates and "twin flames," however, contribute to the idea that people will have instant love connections without having to work to sustain them. Due to the emphasis on the infatuation stage of love in and outside New Age circles, people lose faith in true love once intense relationships unravel. In *All About Love*, hooks laments not only Lil' Kim's disinterest in true love but also the disinterest of ordinary people who told her that true love is a myth.

To experience such love one has to believe in it, with the understanding that true love does not mean a couple will always be together, hooks writes. Should a relationship in which two people truly love each other end, the pair's spiritual connection will continue to enhance their lives. That's because true love, she states, is not just about loving another person; it is about experiencing love in a way that allows for the discovery of one's true self.

If there's a flaw in hooks' discussion of love, it's the story she shares about meeting a true love she first saw in a dream. As her memoir *Bone Black* reveals, dreams played an important role in hooks' life. In that book, she has dreams about her destiny and turns to her maternal grandmother to interpret them. In *All About Love*, hooks recalls a dream so vivid that she felt it had to be a vision of the future. She dreamed that if she attended a conference, she would literally "meet a man of her dreams," a true love.[12] So, she attended the conference, met the man she saw in her dream, and instantly bonded with him, only to discover that he was already in a committed relationship. "I was puzzled and disturbed," she recollects. "I could not believe divine forces in the universe would lead me to this man of my dreams when there was no real possibility of fully realizing those dreams. Of course, those dreams were all about being in a romantic relationship. That was the beginning of a difficult lesson in true love."[13]

Since hooks repeatedly describes true love as a relationship rooted in mutual care, respect, and communication, it is unclear how the man from her dream could have been her true love, as they had no opportunity to develop such a partnership. Still, hooks asserts that her chance meeting with him taught her that true love is not necessarily happily-ever-after love. One may not have a lifelong relationship with a true love, but the love experienced will be "stronger than death."[14]

Not everyone has the courage to enter a true love relationship, especially men, according to hooks. She blames this on patriarchy conditioning men to prefer relationships in which they can control their partners and withhold their emotions over relationships in which both partners have equal footing. Citing books such as John

Stoltenberg's *The End of Manhood: A Book for Men of Conscience* (1993) and Victor Seidler's *Rediscovering Masculinity: Reason, Language and Sexuality* (1989), hooks argues that patriarchy teaches boys and men to create a false self, one who learns to mask his feelings or disconnect from them entirely. Given her belief that "patriarchy has no gender," hooks does not just hold men accountable for socializing boys in this manner but also sexist mothers who teach boys to suppress their emotions. In the end, patriarchal socialization results in men lying to themselves and to relationship partners, using dishonesty to dominate, according to hooks.

"Most men use psychological terrorism as a way to subordinate women," she asserts. "This is a socially acceptable form of coercion. And lying is one of the most powerful weapons in this arsenal."[15] This dishonesty prevents such men from experiencing true love, even though they may crave it—a desire patriarchy teaches men they should not have. The goal of true love, though, is a relationship in which those involved reveal their authentic selves to each other and to themselves, hooks states.

As a survivor of domestic violence, not just as a child but as an adult in a long-term romantic relationship, hooks had years of firsthand experience with emotionally numb men. "This inability to connect with others carries with it an inability to assume responsibility for causing pain," she writes in *All About Love*. "This denial is most evident in cases where men seek to justify extreme violence toward those less powerful, usually women, by suggesting they are the ones who are really victimized by females."[16]

The passage of time has revealed the prescience of the feminist's observations. Dating back to the 1960s and '70s, the men's rights movement existed for decades when hooks wrote *All About Love*, but it was mainly a fringe movement of men asserting that feminism led to their loss of male privilege in society. As *All About Love* appeared on the *New York Times* bestseller list two decades after it was first published, however, men's rights had entered the mainstream buoyed by the rise of social media. Known by many names—incels, red pillers, or "Men Going Their Own Way" (MGTOW)—so-called men's rights activists acquired millions of followers on social networking sites and not just in their lonely corner of the "manosphere." Leaders of these groups became some of the most searched names on the internet and subjects of profiles in the mainstream press in the early 2020s. No longer on the periphery, these leaders shared with the masses their views that real men are those who accumulate wealth, cars, and young attractive women they can dominate. Of course, some of these men, such as those who belong to MGTOW, have decided that they no longer need women at all.

Although racism is also found in men's rights groups, the ideas espoused by these activists cross racial lines, with males of all backgrounds and ages subscribing to their take on capitalist patriarchy. While some of these men acknowledge that they have been hurt by women, they choose to embrace misogyny rather than explore their feelings in depth or acknowledge their need for real love or spiritual connection. In short, hooks does not simply use her own experiences to generalize about men and women in romantic relationships in *All About Love* but identifies behavior that is now widely known as "toxic masculinity." She stresses how this behavior hurts men as well as women.

Additionally, hooks doesn't just blame men for the pervasive lovelessness in society or dishonesty in intimate relationships. Under patriarchy, she notes, women employ dishonesty to gain power over others as well. She references psychologist Harriet Lerner's 1993 book *The Dance of Deception* to challenge women to be transparent in their relationships. hooks writes,

> Indeed, if patriarchal masculinity estranges men from their selfhood, it is equally true that women who embrace patriarchal femininity, the insistence that females should act as though they are weak, incapable of rational thought, dumb, silly, are also socialized to wear a mask—to lie. This is one of the primary themes in Lerner's *The Dance of Deception*. With shrewd insight, she calls women to account for our participation and structures of pretense and lies—particularly within family life.[17]

Instead of openly dominating, women tend to manipulate to get what they want from men or lie to "bolster male self-esteem," according to hooks.[18] When women lie, their dishonesty harms their relationships and reinforces sexist stereotypes about women and deceit that date back to Adam and Eve, hooks writes. Her references to the Bible and Lerner to examine lying, manipulative women are not a coincidence but a reflection of hooks' spiritual vision.

As a feminist of faith, hooks never downplayed her concerns about sexism in Christianity. And as a Buddhist, hooks drew inspiration from both male and female thinkers who were also drawn to the spiritual practice. As a feminist and a Buddhist, Lerner shares hooks' perspective on the purpose of relationships, arguing that they have a deeper role than just romance. "It is in relationships that we discover, enhance and invent the self," Lerner contends. "And it is through working on the self that we enhance our relationships."[19]

In *All About Love*, hooks emphasizes not only love in romantic relationships but also love of the self. Having survived a childhood in which she was abused, shamed, and alienated, hooks spent her adulthood in recovery. She tried to unlearn the harmful messages she received as a child and foster self-esteem through a spiritual practice informed by the teachings of social psychologists and religious leaders dedicated to ending domination. All too often, oppression begins at home, affecting children's relationships with themselves and others well after they grow up. But healthier outcomes are possible, which is why hooks devotes a section of *All About Love* to exploring how parents can raise children with loving-kindness.

FAMILY, FRIENDS, AND SELF

In *All About Love*, hooks urges readers to reconsider whether they grew up in healthy, loving families. She argues, using a definition of love rooted in spiritual growth, that most people did not:

> An overwhelming majority of us come from dysfunctional families in which we were taught we were not okay, where we were shamed, verbally and/or physically abused, and emotionally neglected even as we were also taught to believe that we were loved. For most folks it is

just too threatening to embrace the definition of love that would no longer enable us to see love as present in our families. Too many of us need to cling to a notion of love that either makes abuse acceptable or at least makes it seem that whatever happened was not that bad.[20]

hooks pushes readers to accept the truth about their families, even if it means admitting that they have spent most of their lives in a state of lovelessness. Confronting this reality is necessary for healing, and it took years of therapy and reflection for her to do so. She did not experience authentic love in her immediate family, but she recognized that her maternal grandfather truly loved her. Through her relationship with him, she developed a stronger sense of herself spiritually, an acknowledgement she also makes in *Bone Black*.

Her grandfather's love is one reason hooks raises concerns in *All About Love* about America's emphasis on nuclear families. Without extended kin, she argues, children have upbringings in households where patriarchy thrives: nuclear families allow fathers to have "absolute rule" in households and mothers to have "secondary rule" over children.[21] Isolated from larger networks of kin, nuclear families make women more dependent on one man, and children more dependent on one woman, creating the perfect environment for abuse, hooks asserts. While extended families may also be dysfunctional, the diversity of people within them increases children's chances of bonding with at least one loving adult if their parents aren't loving. Unless children receive more rights in society and grow up with a variety of kin in their lives, many will grow up in loveless homes.

More rights for children include upbringings in homes where adults do not physically abuse them. hooks argues that if it's not okay for men to hit women, then it shouldn't be okay for adults to hit children. Rather than striking children, caregivers need to set boundaries before kids act out and teach them to establish personal codes of conduct. Loving parents make a point to discipline children without punishment as the focus. They teach children to take responsibility for their actions and may revoke a child's privileges as a discipline method among other alternatives to corporal punishment.

In short, their parenting is not based in domination, a toxic family dynamic that men can help change.

"By being giving, by being generous," hooks writes, men can break the cycle of domination and foster love in families. "This is why feminists extolled the virtues of male parenting. Working as caregivers to young children, many men are able to experience for the first time the joy that comes from service."[22]

In the United States, married mothers continue to work a second shift, meaning they do twice as much housework and caregiving as their male partners. Nordic countries enjoy more equity, thanks largely to the region introducing gender-neutral parental leave in the 1970s and '80s. In contrast, it took until the 1990s for the US to introduce parental leave, and it is not guaranteed for all workers.

Initially, most Nordic fathers did not seize the opportunity to stay at home and care for their children, work traditionally demanded of mothers. But "The State of Nordic Fathers," a 2019 survey of 7,515 people from Sweden, Denmark, Iceland, Finland, and Norway, found that Nordic fathers of the twenty-first century are much more enthusiastic about parenting, with 75 percent of such men reporting that they believe parental leave should be split evenly between parents. An equal percentage of women expressed support for shared parental leave. Additionally, 89 percent of Danish men and 96 percent of Swedish men said they felt capable of caregiving and wanted to be very involved in the first months and years of their children's lives.[23]

Male caregivers benefit the entire family. Fathers who take long parental leaves have better relationships with their partners and children than men who do not. They also personally benefit, as the survey found that these fathers report more satisfaction with their lives overall. Perhaps they experience "the joy that comes from service," as hooks puts it. Active fathers also disrupt patriarchy because they tend not to adhere to gender norms or over-rely on their female partners for guidance in caregiving. When they need help, they take the initiative and consult parenting books or doctors, according to "The State of Nordic Fathers."

Nordic men aren't perfect. In Sweden, which in 1974 became the first country to introduce paid parental leave, fathers use under a third of the total time allotted to them to care for their newborns. Still, significant progress has been made by gender-neutral parental leave alone. The policy counteracts the patriarchal norms that contribute to dominance and dysfunction in families.

Toxic and unloving families may be more common than not, but in *All About Love*, hooks rejects the notion that all families are broken. Functional families exist and should be celebrated. In these families, according to hooks, "self-esteem is learned, and there is a balance between autonomy and dependency."[24] She also quotes John Bradshaw's The *Family: A Revolutionary Way of Self Discovery* to make it clear that functional families are those in which all members have functional relationships with each other and are allowed to use "all of their human power."[25]

hooks grew up having strained relationships with family members. As the family misfit, hooks' self-esteem suffered long after she left home for college and entered adulthood. To achieve self-acceptance and silence the rejecting and devaluing voices she'd internalized, she turned to affirmations after her therapist sister suggested they might help. Skeptical at first, hooks began reciting affirmations such as, "I'm breaking with old patterns and moving forward with my life." Repeating the affirmations, she writes, provided "a tremendous energy boost—a way to kick off the day by my accentuating the positive—I also found it useful to repeat them during the day if I felt particularly stressed or was falling into the abyss of negative thinking. Affirmations helped restore my emotional equilibrium."[26]

She credits the feminist movement, and particularly Gloria Steinem's book *The Revolution from Within*, for ingraining in women that they need to achieve more than worldly success but to complete the internal work to build their self-esteem as well. If they do not, they will be successful but self-hating. To develop her self-esteem, hooks modeled her life on Nathaniel Branden's book *Six Pillars of Self-Esteem*. They include the following principles: the practice of living consciously, self-acceptance, self-responsibility, self-assertiveness, living purposefully, and the practice of personal integrity.

In an ideal world, everyone would learn how to love in childhood, hooks writes, but because that rarely happens, individuals seeking wholeness as adults have to take steps to love themselves. To be able to love others, self-love is critical. As hooks explains,

> Self-love is the foundation of our loving practice. Without it our other efforts to love fail. Giving ourselves love we provide our inner being with the opportunity to have the unconditional love we may have always longed to receive from someone else.... We can give ourselves the unconditional love that is the grounding for sustained acceptance and affirmation. When we give this precious gift to ourselves, we are able to reach out to others from a place of fulfillment and not from a place of lack.[27]

hooks is clear that self-love cannot be practiced in isolation, for it is not an easy feat to accomplish. Alone, individuals may feel trapped by the negative voices that devalue and demean them or replay in their heads the traumatic experiences they've already survived. And since hooks' definition of love refers to it as an action for one's own or another person's spiritual growth, it is an inherently relational practice. When people learn to relate to others better by viewing love as a combination of care, trust, respect, knowledge, and responsibility, they can relate to themselves better. They can learn to give themselves the care they give others.

When a person doesn't learn how to give or receive this care in families, they can learn to do so among chosen family, among friends. Typically, in US society, romantic and familial relationships are valued over friendships, depriving people of the healthy lifelong bonds that can form in their chosen families. Among dear friends, people may experience the "redemptive love" and "caring community" they never received in their families of origin, hooks states.[28] Experiencing genuine love among friends also prepares people to love better in their family or romantic relationships.

Since people are taught to devalue friendships in comparison to family and romantic relationships, however, they may miss out on the opportunity to experience authentic love among members of their chosen family. Viewing friendships as secondary to the relationships one has with family members or romantic partners is not without risk. Often, this way of thinking leads people to become socially isolated or dependent on romantic partners, and the risk of this happening is higher if one's romantic relationship is dysfunctional.

In *All About Love*, hooks recalls the emotional devastation she felt when her close friends fell in love and ignored their chosen family. hooks, however, also admits to being in a romantic relationship that she prioritized over her friendships. When the relationship became abusive, she struggled to leave, in part, because she lacked a support network. When she did muster the courage to end the relationship, she was lonely because she no longer had friends. As she aged, hooks learned not to treat romantic partnerships as if they were more important than other personal relationships. She writes,

> There is no special love exclusively reserved for romantic partners. Genuine love is the foundation of our engagement with ourselves, with family, with friends, with partners, with everyone we choose to love. While we will necessarily behave differently depending on the nature of a relationship, or have varying degrees of commitment, the values that inform our behavior, when rooted in the love ethic, are always the same for any interaction.[29]

By treating all relationships as if they're equally valuable, people learn to hold the individuals in their lives to the same standards. hooks writes that she never would have tolerated a friend being physically or emotionally abusive to her, but she tolerated such behavior in a romantic relationship simply because it had been instilled in her that romantic relationships take precedence over friendships. After leaving her romantic relationship, hooks determined that it is more fulfilling to have a circle of love than to depend on a single person, particularly a romantic partner, to fulfill all of one's needs. "Loving friendships," she asserts, "provide us with a space to experience the joy of community in a relationship where we learn to process all our issues, to cope with differences and conflict while staying connected."[30]

Notice that hooks uses the term *loving friendships*. Just as many families are unloving, so are many so-called friendships. People who grew up in dysfunctional families will need to learn what healthy relationships look like before they can form a chosen family that is genuinely loving. If not, they risk choosing friends who are as dysfunctional and withholding as their family members. hooks mentions that the unresolved trauma from her upbringing led her to choose unhealthy partners, but she ignores that people who experience this kind of trauma are vulnerable to connecting with a wide range of unhealthy people in their lives, including purported friends.

Despite this oversight, her points about the importance of friendship stand. If love is the same in any relationship—whether it is with oneself, one's family members, or one's romantic partners—its power does not diminish among friends. Love, as hooks insists, is everything.

All About Love explores how love rooted in one's own or another person's spiritual growth perfects relationships with friends, family, and self. But it is also a book about healing and, more specifically, the healing of bell hooks from a childhood in which she felt profoundly unloved in her nuclear family and an adulthood in which she felt similarly in her romantic relationships. She healed through a spiritual practice informed by humanistic psychology and religious traditions including Catholicism, Protestantism, the Black church, and Buddhism. She healed through daily prayer and belief in prophetic dreams, angels, and true love.

She dared to share her belief system in *All About Love* even if it meant that book reviewers would ridicule her, and her colleagues in the academy, where rational thought is welcomed and spiritual thought met with skepticism, would too. She also shares unpopular opinions rooted in her anticapitalist, antiracist, and antisexist political beliefs: she calls out corporal punishment of children, nuclear families, and how both men and women behave dishonestly in relationships. The risks hooks takes on its pages make *All About Love* an incredibly brave book.

Afterword

All About Love is a guide about love—and death. The book teaches that when people know how to love well, they can also die well. bell hooks strove to "leave folks as though we might never be meeting again," she explains. "This practice makes us change how we talk and interact. It is a way to live consciously."[1] The habit reassured her that she'd die confident that harsh words wouldn't be her last or that heartfelt words wouldn't go unsaid.

Practicing loving-kindness not only leaves individuals without regrets but also allows them to remain connected to their departed loved ones. "Love is the only force that allows us to hold one another close beyond the grave," hooks writes. "When we allow our dead to be forgotten, we fall prey to the notion that the end of embodied life corresponds to the death of the spirit."[2]

hooks took steps to ensure that she would not be forgotten after her death, which took place on December 15, 2021. In addition to writing more than three dozen books that will continue to teach readers about imperialist white supremacist capitalist patriarchy, hooks spearheaded the opening of the bell hooks center at Berea College. The bookshelves contain hooks' work, the columns throughout the center feature famous hooks quotes, and the programming serves queer students, students of color, and other marginalized young people. Launched on September 22, 2021, just months before her death, the center is a space devoted to feminist "scholarship, activism and radical inclusion."[3] Each year, a new class of students will utilize the center, introducing them to hooks' body of work and social impact. Efforts by right-wing politicians to deny young people access to her writing and that of others who acknowledge the reality of oppression make the existence of the bell hooks center even more meaningful.[4]

The censorship of her books would not have surprised hooks. Her observations in 2006's *Homegrown* about art, access, and education all apply to today's climate:

Art-making provides a process for us to explore our life experiences—including the experiences of prejudice, racism, and homophobia—and make them public. It follows that art is now perceived differently than before—it is seen as a vehicle for change, as a force that can break down the boundaries and expose inequalities. So, people of color and the poor are denied access to art for fear that if they get their hands on it, they'll write their own stories and understand the value of their lives. Let's expand that, not just to art, but to education as a whole.[5]

hooks' own political awakening occurred as a first-year college student reading the autobiography *of Malcolm X*, she reveals in *Homegrown*. Since much of the change that has taken place on college campuses directly results from Black people insisting on access to education, "it's no accident we have a backlash," hooks asserts. "And today, there's not only an assault on affirmative action but on women's studies, Black studies, Chicana studies, and so forth."[6]

In 2023, when the Supreme Court ended affirmative action, and a movement against the teaching of race, gender, sexuality, and current events in schools left almost no state untouched, hooks' words proved prophetic. When she writes in *Appalachian Elegy* about "the spiritual power of black people," those who have the uncanny ability to "carry messages from the future,"[7] she does not just describe her elders but herself.

But that didn't stop publishers from suggesting her style of writing was outdated after her popularity waned in the aughts.[8] She believed such slights were rooted in both ageism and sexism, pointing out that men don't lose their "cool" factor as they age, a privilege denied to women.[9] The idea that she lost relevance is contradicted by the fact that recordings of her panel discussions throughout the 2010s have netted tens of thousands of online page views. *All About Love*'s appearance on the *New York Times* bestseller list shortly before her death is another indication that people across generations remain interested in her thoughts. hooks' concerns about the commodification of feminism, the hypersexualization of Black women, the nefarious influence of capitalism, and religious fundamentalism are pressing issues two years after her death and decades after she first raised these issues.

"Stan culture," or the public's overidentification with the rich and famous, is an insidious offshoot of capitalism that's only intensified since Eminem's song "Stan" gave rise to the term in 2000. Despite the politicization of fourth-wave feminism during Trump's journey to the White House, the movement and its associated spirituality continues to be marketed as a lifestyle. Social media images of women in flowing garments surrounded by crystals, sometimes posting political hashtags but mostly selling "spiritual" services, attest to this. Meanwhile, fundamentalists continue to repress women and girls globally. In countries such as Iran and Afghanistan, Islamic extremists deny female citizens access to healthcare, education, free speech, and due process. In the United States, the religious right pervades politics at all levels, from the school board to the Supreme Court. They're influencing what students do with their minds and what women and trans people do with their bodies.

Since hooks' 1997 interview with Lil' Kim, a proliferation of Black women reciting sexually explicit lyrics have entered, and even dominated, the music industry. This trend has coincided with an uptick of Black women feeling pressure to cosmetically enhance their backsides in a misguided bid to become modern-day Hottentot Venuses. Popular hip-hop model Angela White, more well known by her former stage name Blac Chyna, made headlines in March 2023 for bucking this trend by undergoing procedures to reduce or remove enhancements she made to her breasts, butt, and face to achieve what had been her signature provocative look. Many of White's young fans applauded her decision, which followed her baptism, and hooks likely would have taken interest in the model's "makeunder" and the message it sent to impressionable girls, too. White also announced that she was leaving OnlyFans, a site that allows users to earn money by sharing sexually explicit content.

As Black women are hypersexualized, they are also hyperinvisibilized. hooks observes the trend in *Homegrown*: "If you look at the trajectory of young, Black (or ethnically indeterminate—Black female bodies have practically disappeared from the screen) female bodies, the biracial body is idealized. The light-skinned colored woman with long straight hair is identified by patriarchal pornographers as the ideal sex object."[10]

hooks longed for the day when Black women would not be portrayed as "whores" or "bitches" but as divine.[11] That day has yet to come.

The ongoing dehumanization and devaluation of Black women caused hooks to worry that after she died, her work would be dismissed and maybe even destroyed, a fate that befell noted Black American scholars before her. That fear impelled her to use her own resources to fund the bell hooks center. For taking charge of her legacy, she faced criticism from detractors who questioned if her intellectual contributions warranted preservation in an academic institution. Their doubts made her feel once again that she was being asked, as she had been as a young woman, "Nigger gal . . . who do you think you are?"[12] But hooks was undeterred.

While she engineered the formation of the bell hooks center, family, friends, faculty, and fans made a concerted effort to remember her through a series of acts following her death. First came the obituaries. Rebecca Walker—a pioneer of the third-wave feminist movement and daughter of second-wave feminist Alice Walker—wrote in the *Los Angeles Times* that hooks was "one of the mighty fires in which I was forged."[13] That reference recalls the fire of the lost spirits that hooks describes dreaming of in *Bone Black*. One of hooks' roles in this world, according to her grandmother Saru, was "making the story, making the words, making the new fire."[14]

Just as Saru told hooks that being a storyteller was her fate, hooks was the first person to identify Walker as a "real writer."[15] Throughout her remembrance of hooks, Walker continues the fire comparison and weaves in religious allusions, too. As a radical Black woman who could be "both demon and demon slayer" or "beautiful and bewitching," Walker writes, hooks "burned it all to the ground," even those ideas that others held sacred.[16] Her spiritual practice informed her criticism, which she believed was "a form of love, an expression of hope, an act of faith," a reference, of course, to 1 Corinthians 13:13.[17]

A woman of contradictions, hooks could be Christlike. She "transformed a wound of passion into a quest for communion," according to Walker.[18] And her modest house atop a Kentucky hill was filled with "Buddhas and African sculptures, magic chests," all symbols of her religious syncretism.[19]

As hooks lay dying, Buddhism comforted her. Walker played a chant for her called "Namo Avalokiteshvara" recorded by monks under the guidance of Thích Nhất Hạnh. The chant, hooks' friend Beth Feagan explains in her remembrance of the feminist, "means by getting in touch with our suffering, the suffering of our parents and ancestors, and the suffering of the world, we can open our hearts to love and compassion."[20] As hooks' family, friends, and caregivers rotated shifts to sit with her on her final day, the chant played repeatedly. A lecturer of general studies at Berea College, Feagan writes that Hạnh's teachings, particularly his book *The Art of Living*, freed hooks from the fear of death. The book includes meditations for happiness and peace; it teaches readers how to grapple with aging and death with curiosity and joy instead of terror.

The Buddhist chant comforted hooks, but Feagan also wanted her to hear familiar spirituals, so she sang "I'll Fly Away," "Wade in the Water," "Swing Low, Sweet Chariot," and "Go Down Moses," among other selections. In recognition, hooks turned her head toward Feagan and tried to open her eyes, Feagan recollected, but the pain medicine in the dying scholar's system prevented her from reacting more strongly.[21]

While Walker remembered hooks as a brilliant and complicated woman, Feagan remembered hooks on her deathbed, weak but still responsive to cherished music. Kentucky writer Silas House, on the other hand, recalled hooks partly as someone who "often wept."[22]

That detail reminds one of Gloria Jean Watkins, the depressed girl in *Bone Black* who constantly burst into tears. As a youth, hooks grieved because of the pain she experienced integrating a white high school where students and teachers alike resented the influx of Black students. And she grieved because she felt like the family misfit. Even in her sixties, she discussed her painful childhood, particularly her troubled relationship with her father.

In 2017, hooks described the sorrow that washed over her when observing the "tremendous" love that a white male lawyer friend showed to his daughters. "It triggered in me profound grief about the fact that I had not had such a father love," she said. "And I began to think, 'Well, what could I have been? Who could I have been had I been loved in that way?' . . . But it allowed me to bring up that grief and to work with it and to heal it."[23]

In autobiographical texts, however, hooks makes it clear that she became a feminist precisely because of her dysfunctional patriarchal family. She learned to resist her father's domination as a child, and she also became a high achiever, winning prizes, excelling on the debate team, mastering manners and etiquette, and standing out for her book smarts. "I was going to be a gifted, talented person on all fronts," she recalls in *Homegrown*.[24]

Had she grown up in a different environment, one in which she had a father like her lawyer friend, it's not certain that hooks would've become a highly decorated writer and scholar—an American Book Award winner, Kentucky Writers Hall of Fame inductee, and Ivy League professor. And she surely would not have spent her career healing from her upbringing and teaching others how to heal right along with her—combining psychology, mysticism, Buddhism, Christianity, and social action to become self-actualized.

Perhaps hooks would have traded all her accolades for a loving father and harmonious family life, but the adult she grew into would not have been the radical feminist obsessed with love and intrigued by death.

hooks had imagined her death in detail years before it occurred. In her 2008 book *Belonging: A Culture of Place*, hooks writes that she was pleased by the idea of dying in her native Kentucky. Just as she and her ecofeminist friends had performed a ritual for her mother in the Kentucky hills, hooks envisioned her own ashes being scattered on a favorite hill there as if "they are seeds and not ash, a burnt offering on solid ground vulnerable to the wind and rain—all that is left of my body gone, my being shifted, passed away, moving forward, and on and into eternity."[25]

Thanks to her vast body of work, the outgrowth of a disciplined spiritual practice, her thoughts and words also live on. They, too, are more like seeds than ash. They plant new ideas in the minds of young and old readers alike, causing them to rethink race, religion, gender, and love. When readers put hooks' ideas to use, they resurrect her. As she writes in *All About Love*, "Sometimes we invoke the dead by allowing wisdom they have shared to guide our present actions."[26]

hooks' wisdom served as a guide when scholars joined together for symposiums to discuss her writing after her death. She is invoked by the mural on the wall of the Christian County Historical Society in her hometown of Hopkinsville and another such mural in Berea. And she was invoked by the month-long celebration of her life, starting with the proclamation of Gloria Watkins Day at the start of Women's History Month 2022, in Hopkinsville. As she is remembered by those activities and in this book she lives.

Writing *bell hooks' Spiritual Vision*, I often had to remind myself that this provocative and charismatic feminist had actually died. As I watched her series of talks at the New School and St. Norbert College, listened to her radio interviews, and read her passionate commentary in essays and books, I found myself nodding along to her observations, smiling at her sense of humor, and at times—as she was wont to do—"talking back." As I remembered her through these appearances and my own recollection of meeting her so long ago, bell hooks' presence felt electric.

In *Belonging* she leaves no doubt about the power of remembering the dead. "Memories," she states, "offer us a world where there is no death, where we are sustained by rituals of regard and recollection."[27]

Notes

CHAPTER ONE

1 bell hooks, *Feminism Is for Everybody: Passionate Politics* (New York: Routledge, 2015), 1.

2 bell hooks, *Ain't I a Woman: Black Women and Feminism* (Boston: South End Press, 1981), 53.

3 Clyde McGrady, "Why bell hooks Didn't Capitalize Her Name," *Washington Post*, December 15, 2021, https://tinyurl.com/3crr436m.

4 Michael Phillips, "bell hooks," Kentucky to the World, https://tinyurl.com/4r8u27k2.

5 Alicia Lee, "Martin Luther King Jr. Explains the Meaning of Love in Rare Handwritten Note," CNN, February 9, 2020, https://tinyurl.com/6r9xh33n.

6 M. Scott Peck, *The Road Less Traveled: A New Psychology of Love, Traditional Values, and Spiritual Growth* (New York: Simon and Schuster, 1978), 83.

7 Peck, *The Road Less Traveled*, 83.

8 Hari Sreenivasan, Sam Weber, and Connie Kargbo, "The True Story behind the 'Welfare Queen' Stereotype," PBS News Hour, June 1, 2019, https://tinyurl.com/bdh32hyn.

9 Sreenivasan, Weber, and Kargbo, "True Story."

10 Allison Graves, "Did Hillary Clinton Call African-American Youth 'Super-predators?,'" Politifact, August 28, 2016, https://tinyurl.com/2p9sm7d2.

11 Sreenivasan, Weber, and Kargbo, "True Story."

12 George Yancy and bell hooks, "bell hooks: Buddhism, the Beats and Loving Blackness," *New York Times*, December 10, 2015, https://tinyurl.com/7tmkhafy.

13 Yancy and hooks, "bell hooks."

14 Yancy and hooks, "bell hooks."

15 bell hooks and Thích Nhất Hạnh, "Building a Community of Love: bell hooks and Thích Nhất Hạnh," *Lion's Roar*, March 24, 2017, https://tinyurl.com/ye2anhkh.

16 hooks and Hạnh, "Building a Community of Love."

17 hooks and Hạnh, "Building a Community of Love."

18 "When Giants Meet," Thích Nhất Hạnh Foundation, January 11, 2017, https://tinyurl.com/5p2s2j6h.

19 "When Giants Meet."

20 "When Giants Meet."

21 "When Giants Meet."

22 "What Is Buddhism?," *Tricycle: The Buddhist Review*, https://tinyurl .com/mv3ume7y.

23 bell hooks, "Toward a Worldwide Culture of Love," *Lion's Roar*, November 8, 2022, https://tinyurl.com/5wvhbj7w.

24 hooks, "Toward a Worldwide Culture."

25 hooks, "Toward a Worldwide Culture."

26 Robert Ham, "Alumna bell hooks—Celebrated Feminist Theorist, Cultural Critic, Artist, and Writer—Dies at 69," The Humanities Institute, UC Santa Cruz, January 6, 2022, https://tinyurl.com/mvuvskbd.

27 bell hooks, "Are You Still a Slave? Liberating the Black Female Body," Eugene Lang College of Liberal Arts at The New School, May 6, 2014, YouTube video, 1:55:32, https://tinyurl.com/msvaumfr.

28 Linda Blackford, "'The World Is a Lesser Place Today without Her.' Acclaimed Author bell hooks Dies at 69," *Lexington Herald Leader*, December 15, 2021, https://tinyurl.com/yf89bx2d.

29 LaRyssa D. Herrington, "A Sacrament of Love: Black Catholic Reflections on the Life and Legacy of bell hooks," *National Catholic Reporter*, June 18, 2022, https://tinyurl.com/nnb3hxnm.

30 bell hooks, *All About Love: New Visions* (New York: HarperCollins Publishers, 2001), 82.

31 hooks, *All About Love*, 82.

32 hooks, *All About Love*, 82.

33 Yancy and hooks, "bell hooks."

34 "The Christian Identity of Berea College," Berea College, https://tinyurl.com/mr94wyet.

35 Yancy and hooks, "bell hooks."

36 Helen Tworkov, "Agent of Change: An Interview with bell hooks," *Tricycle: The Buddhist Review*, Fall 1992, https://tinyurl.com/3n9d64u9.

37 hooks and Hạnh, "Building a Community of Love."

38 hooks, "Are You Still a Slave?"

39 hooks, "Are You Still a Slave?"

40 hooks, "Are You Still a Slave?"

41 hooks, "Are You Still a Slave?"

42 hooks, "Are You Still a Slave?"

43 hooks, *All About Love*, 175.

44 Amalia Mesa-Bains and bell hooks, *Homegrown: Engaged Cultural Criticism* (New York: Taylor & Francis, 2017), 23.

45 Mesa-Bains and hooks, *Homegrown*, 23.

46 bell hooks, "Beyoncé's Lemonade Is Capitalist Money-Making at Its Best," *Guardian*, May 11, 2016, https://tinyurl.com/22ydkrrc.

47 Carol McColgin, "Beyonce's Stylist B. Akerlund on Finding the Perfect Yellow Dress for 'Lemonade,'" Hollywood Reporter, April 25, 2016, https://tinyurl.com/23jtf6wt.

48 hooks, "Beyoncé's Lemonade."

49 hooks and Hạnh, "Building a Community of Love."

50 bell hooks and Gloria Steinem, "bell hooks & Gloria Steinem at Eugene Lang College," Eugene Lang College of Liberal Arts at The New School, October 8, 2014, YouTube video, 1:45:29, https://tinyurl.com/2wn4aadt.

51 Tworkov, "Agent of Change."

52 hooks, "Beyoncé's Lemonade."

53 hooks, "Beyoncé's Lemonade."

54 Tworkov, "Agent of Change."

55 Raylene Chang, "Characteristics of the Self-Actualized Person: Visions from the East and West," Counseling & Values 36, no. 1 (October 1991): 2–10.

56 hooks, "Beyoncé's Lemonade."

57 Hillary Crosley Coker, "What bell hooks Really Means When She Calls Beyoncé a 'Terrorist,'" Jezebel, May 9, 2014, https://tinyurl.com/3dvsdbbv.

58 bell hooks, Black Looks: Race and Representation (Boston: South End Press, 1992), 164.

59 hooks, All About Love, 27.

60 bell hooks, "Spike Lee's Malcom X," Artforum, February 1993, https://tinyurl.com/bdf2bmzj.

61 hooks, "Spike Lee's Malcom X."

62 hooks, "Spike Lee's Malcom X."

63 hooks, "Beyoncé's Lemonade."

64 hooks, "Spike Lee's Malcom X."

65 hooks, "Spike Lee's Malcom X."

66 hooks, "Beyoncé's Lemonade."

67 bell hooks, "Hardcore Honey: bell hooks Goes on the Down Low with Lil' Kim," Paper, May 1997, https://tinyurl.com/yuyrzjzz.

68 "bell hooks and the Sour 'Lemonade' Review," Ebony, May 11, 2016, https://tinyurl.com/26jdn99r.

69 Julie Zeilinger, "Emma Watson and bell hooks Talk Hermione, Beyoncé and Why Feminism Is for Everybody," Mic, February 22, 2016, https://tinyurl.com/j7n5jm25.

70 Mikki Kendall, "bell hooks Pushed Us to Think Harder About Feminism, Black Women and Beyoncé," Washington Post, December 16, 2021, https://tinyurl.com/8mwkzsdk.

71 "Formation," track 12 on Beyoncé, Lemonade, Parkwood Entertainment LLC and Columbia Records, 2016.

72 Jennifer Schuessler, The Wide-Angle Vision, and Legacy, of bell hooks," New York Times, December 20, 2021, https://www.nytimes.com/2021/12/16/books/bell-hooks-black-women-feminism.html.

73 Lynnée Denise (@lynneedenise), "I don't like the mean-spirited protection of Beyoncé," Twitter, August 3, 2022, https://tinyurl.com/2p8fzctk.
74 Clay Risen, "bell hooks, Pathbreaking Black Feminist, Dies at 69," *New York Times*, December 15, 2021, https://tinyurl.com/2afdjhfr.
75 Tworkov, "Agent of Change."

CHAPTER TWO

1   bell hooks, *Bone Black: Memories of Girlhood* (New York: Henry Holt and Co., 1996), xii.
2   Risen, "bell hooks, Pathbreaking Black Feminist."
3   hooks, *Bone Black*, 87.
4   Joy DeGruy, *Post Traumatic Slave Syndrome: America's Legacy of Enduring Injury and Healing* (Stone Mountain, GA: Joy DeGruy Publications Inc., 2017), 229.
5   hooks, *Bone Black*, 130.
6   hooks, *Bone Black*, 30.
7   James Cone, *God of the Oppressed* (New York: Seabury Press, 1975), 105.
8   "Obituary: Toni Morrison," BBC News, August 6, 2019, https://tinyurl.com/4225sd6x.
9   bell hooks and Parker J. Palmer, "bell hooks and Parker J. Palmer dialogue at St. Norbert College," St. Norbert College, April 26, 2016, YouTube video, 1:41:56, https://tinyurl.com/3ukwy78y.
10 hooks, *Bone Black*, 146.
11 hooks, *Bone Black*, 146.
12 hooks, *Bone Black*, 41.
13 hooks, *Bone Black*, 14.
14 hooks, *Bone Black*, 120.
15 hooks, *Bone Black*, 120.
16 hooks, *All About Love*, 20.
17 R. L. Stollar, "Love Does Not Abuse: The Parenting Philosophy of bell hooks," *R. L. Stollar* (blog), December 6, 2020, https://tinyurl.com/4umf2y4x.
18 bell hooks and Kevin Powell, "bell hooks and Kevin Powell: Black Masculinity, Threat or Threatened," Eugene Lang College of Liberal Arts at The New School, October 7, 2015, YouTube video, 1:39:04, https://tinyurl.com/yc65fyvv.
19 hooks, *Bone Black*, 32.
20 Stollar, "Love Does Not Abuse."
21 Matt 20:16 KJV.
22 hooks, *Bone Black*, 32.
23 Exod 20:12 NIRV.
24 Guida C. Eldorado, "'Spare the Rod, Spoil the Child' Isn't Biblical," *Chicago Tribune*, March 13, 2005, https://tinyurl.com/awtdcmaf.
25 hooks, *Bone Black*, 5.

26 hooks, *Bone Black*, 44.
27 hooks, *Bone Black*, 44.
28 hooks, *Bone Black*, 44.
29 hooks, *Bone Black*, 45.
30 "Fast Facts: Preventing Adverse Childhood Experiences," Centers for Disease Control and Prevention, April 6, 2022, https://tinyurl.com/ydpx77jx.
31 bell hooks, "bell hooks in an Open Dialogue with New School Students—Whose Booty Is This?" Eugene Lang College of Liberal Arts at The New School, October 10, 2014, YouTube video, 1:21:12, https://tinyurl.com/5fbxjn4m.
32 hooks, *Bone Black*, 55.
33 hooks, *Bone Black*, 56.
34 hooks, *Bone Black*, 56.
35 hooks, *Bone Black*, 56.
36 hooks, *Bone Black*, 45.
37 hooks, *Bone Black*, 56.
38 hooks, *Bone Black*, 64.
39 hooks, *Bone Black*, 65.
40 hooks, *Bone Black*, 85.
41 hooks, *Bone Black*, 85.
42 hooks, *Bone Black*, 87.
43 hooks, *Bone Black*, 89.
44 hooks and Powell, "bell hooks and Kevin Powell."

CHAPTER THREE

1 hooks, *Bone Black*, 85.
2 hooks, *Bone Black*, 158.
3 hooks, *Bone Black*, 45.
4 hooks, *Bone Black*, 71.
5 hooks, *Bone Black*, 71.
6 hooks, *Bone Black*, 71.
7 hooks, *Bone Black*, 72.
8 hooks, *Bone Black*, 74.
9 hooks, *Feminism Is for Everybody*, 101.
10 hooks, *Bone Black*, 75.
11 hooks, *Bone Black*, 80.
12 hooks, *Bone Black*, 80.
13 hooks, *Bone Black*, 128.
14 hooks, *Bone Black*, 134–35.
15 hooks, *Bone Black*, 77.
16 hooks, *Bone Black*, 57.
17 hooks, *Bone Black*, 49.
18 hooks, *Bone Black*, 50, 3.

19 bell hooks, *Yearning: Race, Gender, and Cultural Politics*, 2nd ed. (New York: Routledge, 2015), 120.

20 hooks, *Bone Black*, 59.

21 hooks, *Bone Black*, 53.

22 hooks, *Bone Black*, 53.

23 hooks, *Bone Black*, 117.

24 hooks, *Bone Black*, 116.

25 hooks, *Bone Black*, 57.

26 Katrina Hazzard-Donald, *Mojo Workin': The Old African American Hoodoo System* (Urbana: University of Illinois Press, 2013), 4.

27 Hazzard-Donald, *Mojo Workin'*, 4.

28 Hazzard-Donald, *Mojo Workin'*, 2.

29 hooks and Powell, "bell hooks and Kevin Powell."

30 Margalit Fox, "Lawrence McKiver, a Singer in Long Tradition, Dies at 97," *New York Times*, April 1, 2013, https://tinyurl.com/mr3pmdds.

31 hooks, *Bone Black*, 73.

32 Hazzard-Donald, *Mojo Workin'*, 7.

33 hooks, *Bone Black*, 86.

34 hooks, *Bone Black*, 170.

35 hooks, *Bone Black*, 170.

36 hooks, *Bone Black*, 3.

37 hooks, *Bone Black*, 170.

38 Gen 16:11–12 KJV.

39 Amy R. Buckley, "In the Midst of the Mess: Hagar and the God Who Sees," CBE International, June 5, 2013, https://tinyurl.com/cfecaw8s.

40 hooks, *Bone Black*, 87.

41 hooks, *Bone Black*, 172–73.

42 hooks, *Bone Black*, 173.

43 hooks, *Bone Black*, 176.

44 Cathy Warner, "In the Wilderness with John the Baptist," *Cathy Warner* (blog), December 8, 2019, https://tinyurl.com/mvw68sf4.

45 Isa 40:3 NKJV; Luke 3:4 NKJV.

46 hooks, *Bone Black*, 177.

47 hooks, *Bone Black*, 183.

48 hooks, *Bone Black*, 111.

49 hooks, *Bone Black*, 175.

CHAPTER FOUR

1 hooks, *Feminism Is for Everybody*, 108.

2 hooks, *Feminism Is for Everybody*, 105.

3 hooks, *Feminism Is for Everybody*, 106.

4 hooks, *Feminism Is for Everybody*, 105.

5   "Who Is Julian of Norwich," Julian of Norwich, https://tinyurl.com/2jpx6ejs.

6   "Who Is Julian of Norwich."

7   "Who Is Julian of Norwich."

8   hooks, *Feminism Is for Everybody*, 105.

9   Nadra Nittle, *Toni Morrison's Spiritual Vision: Faith, Folktales, and Feminism in Her Life and Literature* (Minneapolis: Fortress Press, 2021), 79.

10   Mesa-Bains and hooks, *Homegrown*, 22.

11   "Beyond the Veil: Spiritualism in the 19th Century," O'Henry Museum, Austin, Texas, https://tinyurl.com/35pt5ezv.

12   Dianca London Potts, "Holy Spirits: The Power and Legacy of America's Female Spiritualists," Shondaland, October 10, 2018, https://tinyurl.com/yck48tz7.

13   Martha Weinman Lear, "The Second Feminist Wave: What Do These Women Want?," *New York Times*, March 10, 1968, https://tinyurl.com/ywm5x2jb.

14   Gloria Steinem, "Scholars, Witches and Other Freedom Fighters," Salem State College, March 1, 1993, https://tinyurl.com/22p85wfm.

15   Jim Doyle, "Earth Mother—Author Starhawk Is a Spiritual Leader for Bay Area Witches," *San Francisco Chronicle*, October 29, 2004, https://tinyurl.com/h7d3puyc.

16   Pam Grossman, "Starhawk, Spiral Goddess," December 7, 2022, in *The Witch Wave*, podcast audio, December 7, 2022, https://tinyurl.com/59s8vnt5.

17   Grossman, "Starhawk, Spiral Goddess."

18   Grossman, "Starhawk, Spiral Goddess."

19   Alice Walker, *In Search of Our Mothers' Gardens: Womanist Prose* (New York: Harcourt, 1983), 14.

20   bell hooks, "This Ain't No P—y S—t," The New School, Eugene Lang College of Liberal Arts at The New School, October 12, 2015, YouTube video, 1:52:12, https://tinyurl.com/3ubcwjau.

21   hooks, "This Ain't No P—y S—t."

22   "Black Women & The Suffrage Movement: 1848–1923," Wesleyan University, https://tinyurl.com/yc6735mr.

23   Laurie Johnston, "Women's Group to Observe Rights Day Here Today," *New York Times*, August 25, 1972, https://tinyurl.com/2scxjvwh.

24   hooks, *Ain't I a Woman*, 31.

25   hooks, *Ain't I a Woman*, 31.

26   hooks, *Ain't I a Woman*, 33.

27   hooks, *Ain't I a Woman*, 85.

28   hooks, *Ain't I a Woman*, 36.

29   Jennifer Katz et al., "White Female Bystanders' Responses to a Black Woman at Risk for Incapacitated Sexual Assault," *Psychology of Women Quarterly* 41, no. 2 (February 10, 2017): 273–85, https://tinyurl.com/48xydby7.

30   bell hooks, "Dig Deep: Beyond Lean In," *Feminist Wire*, October 28, 2013.

31   hooks and Steinem, "bell hooks & Gloria Steinem."

32 Mimi Albert, "Luisah Teish—Yoruba Priestess, Psychic Channel, Storyteller, Shaman—Describes Her Return to the Goddesses and Gods of Her West African Spiritual Roots," *Yoga Journal*, January/February 1987, https://tinyurl.com/2vksc56m.

33 Luisah Teish, *Jambalaya: The Natural Woman's Book of Personal Charms & Practical Rituals* (San Francisco: Harper & Row, 1988), 171.

34 Teish, *Jambalaya*.

35 Albert, "Luisah Teish."

36 hooks, *Feminism Is for Everybody*, 106.

37 hooks, *Feminism Is for Everybody*, 106.

38 hooks, *Feminism Is for Everybody*, 108.

39 Laura Nagel, "Margot Adler," Dictionary of Unitarian and Universalist Biography, December 3, 2016, https://tinyurl.com/54c47rsh.

40 bell hooks, *Appalachian Elegy* (Lexington: University of Kentucky Press, 2012), 7.

41 hooks, *Appalachian Elegy*, 70.

42 hooks, *Ain't I a Woman*, 30.

43 hooks, *Feminism Is for Everybody*, 107.

44 hooks, *Feminism Is for Everybody*, 107.

45 hooks, *Feminism Is for Everybody*, 107–8.

46 hooks, *Yearning*, 35.

47 Debra Walker King, "Alice Walker's Jesus: A Womanist Paradox," Forum on Public Policy, https://tinyurl.com/3jnc3u5d.

48 bell hooks, *Sisters of the Yam: Black Women and Self-Recovery* (New York: Routledge, 2015), 170.

49 hooks, *Sisters of the Yam*, 170.

50 Ada María Isasi-Díaz, "Mujeristas: A Name of Our Own!!," *Christian Century, May 24–31, 1989*, 560, https://tinyurl.com/5n72esjx.

51 Grossman, "Starhawk, Spiral Goddess."

52 Grossman, "Starhawk, Spiral Goddess."

CHAPTER FIVE

1 Sara M. Moniuszko, "What's the Deal with WitchTok? We Spoke to Creators Bringing Magic to TikTok," *USA Today*, October 14, 2021, https://tinyurl.com/37pf4ebt.

2 "Modeling the Future of Religion in America," Pew Research Center, September 13, 2022, https://tinyurl.com/mryreua5.

3 hooks, *Feminism Is for Everybody*, 109.

4 Nadra Nittle, "The Occult Is Having a Moment. Companies Want in, but Not If Witches Can Help It," Vox, October 31, 2018, https://tinyurl.com/2crbdbmj.

5 Margot Adler, *Drawing Down the Moon* (New York: Penguin Books, 2006), 239.

6 hooks, "Dig Deep."

7 hooks, "Dig Deep."

8 hooks, "Dig Deep."

9 hooks and Steinem, "bell hooks & Gloria Steinem."

10 hooks, *Feminism Is for Everybody*, 110.

11 hooks and Steinem, "bell hooks & Gloria Steinem."

12 hooks and Steinem, "bell hooks & Gloria Steinem."

13 hooks and Steinem, "bell hooks & Gloria Steinem."

14 German Lopez, "Donald Trump Said It's Okay to Call Women 'Fat Pigs, Dogs, Slobs, and Disgusting Animals,' Vox, August 6, 2015, https://tinyurl.com/2czy36k6.

15 Libby Nelson, "Grab 'Em by the P—y": How Trump Talked About Women In Private Is Horrifying," Vox, October 7, 2016, https://tinyurl.com/2pjd8fc7; Eliza Relman, "The 26 Women Who Have Accused Trump of Sexual Misconduct," Insider, September 17, 2020, https://tinyurl.com/va4jyfu5.

16 bell hooks, George Yancy, and Harry Brod, "'Feminist Future: Mutual Dialogue' featuring bell hooks, George Yancy and Harry Brod," St. Norbert College, April 11, 2017, YouTube video, 1:46:06, https://tinyurl.com/4t5kvt6a.

17 Alix Langone, "Brooklyn Witches Plan to Put a Hex on Supreme Court Justice Brett Kavanaugh," *Time*, October 14, 2018, https://tinyurl.com/yckneu32.

18 Langone, "Brooklyn Witches Plan to Put a Hex."

19 Emma Grey Ellis, "Trump's Presidency Has Spawned a New Generation of Witches," Wired, October 30, 2019, https://tinyurl.com/5bha43wc.

20 Heather Greene, "How to Make a Thousand Witches with One Supreme Court Decision," Religion News Service, June 6, 2022, https://tinyurl.com/3jn432zp.

21 Tara Isabella Burton, "Each Month, Thousands of Witches Cast a Spell against Donald Trump," Vox, October 30, 2017, https://tinyurl.com/52phps2m.

22 Mesa-Bains and hooks, *Homegrown*, 10.

23 Mesa-Bains and hooks, *Homegrown*, 1.

24 Mesa-Bains and hooks, *Homegrown*, 2.

25 Nadine White, "Catholic Church Unveils Black Mary and Jesus Posters in Anti-racism Drive," *Independent*, February 6, 2023, https://tinyurl.com/4uy6p2ja.

26 hooks and Steinem, "bell hooks & Gloria Steinem."

27 hooks and Steinem, "bell hooks & Gloria Steinem."

28 Benjamin Genocchio, "Unraveling a Complex Imagery," *New York Times*, August 28, 2005, https://tinyurl.com/3f8umb6w.

29 hooks and Steinem, "bell hooks & Gloria Steinem."

30 Mesa-Bains and hooks, *Homegrown*, 65.

31 Mesa-Bains and hooks, *Homegrown*, 14.

32 Mesa-Bains and hooks, *Homegrown*, 99

33 Mesa-Bains and hooks, *Homegrown*, 116.

34 Mesa-Bains and hooks, *Homegrown*, 115.

35 Mesa-Bains and hooks, *Homegrown*, 116.

36 Nadra Nittle, "Betye Saar: The Brilliant Artist Who Reversed and Radicalised Racist Stereotypes," *Guardian*, September 23, 2021, https://tinyurl.com/2p8tyy6h.

37 Mesa-Bains and hooks, *Homegrown*, 125.

38 Mesa-Bains and hooks, *Homegrown*, 125.

39 Mesa-Bains and hooks, *Homegrown*, 126.

40 hooks, *Sisters of the Yam*, 1.

41 hooks, *Sisters of the Yam*, 1.

42 hooks, *Sisters of the Yam*, 2.

43 hooks, *Sisters of the Yam*, 2.

44 hooks, *Sisters of the Yam*, 2.

45 hooks, *Sisters of the Yam*, 1.

46 hooks, *Sisters of the Yam*, 143–44.

47 hooks, *Sisters of the Yam*, 171.

48 hooks, *Sisters of the Yam*, 169.

49 hooks, *Sisters of the Yam*, 165.

50 hooks, *Sisters of the Yam*, 174.

CHAPTER SIX

1 Elise Harris, "That 4-Letter Word," *New York Times*, January 30, 2000, https://tinyurl.com/2p97ekzy.

2 Harris, "That 4-Letter Word."

3 hooks, *All About Love*, 19.

4 Harris, "That 4-Letter Word."

5 hooks, *All About Love*, 229.

6 hooks, *All About Love*, 230–31.

7 Harris, "That 4-Letter Word."

8 Harris, "That 4-Letter Word."

9 Dan Kois, "A Totally Normal Interview with Author Emily St. John Mandel," Slate, December 17, 2022, https://tinyurl.com/2beatknj.

10 Joshunda Sanders, "Remembering bell hooks: Healing Occurs through Testimony," Oprah Daily, December 16, 2021, https://tinyurl.com /yc6ue8tv.

11 "Census Bureau Releases New Estimates on America's Families and Living Arrangement," United States Census Bureau, November 17, 2022, https://tinyurl.com/ymzcmk4n.

12 Dana Goldstein and Robert Gebeloff, "As Gen X and Boomers Age, They Confront Living Alone," *New York Times*, November 27, 2022, https://tinyurl.com/y3t946dz.

13 hooks, Yancy, and Brod, "Feminist Future: Mutual Dialogue."

14 Wendy L. Patrick, "Why Many Single Women without Children Are So Happy," *Psychology Today*, February 28, 2021, https://tinyurl.com/bdzasj27.

15 hooks, *All About Love*, 140.

16 Greg Matos, "What's Behind the Rise of Lonely, Single Men," *Psychology Today*, August 9, 2022, https://tinyurl.com/bdfrtm84.

17 Yancy and bell hooks, "hooks."

18 Lynnée Denise, "Appreciation: Here's What We All Owe bell hooks, Beginning with Me," *Los Angeles Times*, December 18, 2021, https://tinyurl.com/23kw7tz5.

19 Colleen Walsh, "Young Adults Hardest Hit by Loneliness During Pandemic," Harvard Gazette, February 17, 2021, https://tinyurl.com/ym8p9aby.

20 Jamie Ballard, "Millennials Are the Loneliest Generation," YouGov America, July 30, 2019, https://tinyurl.com/2rapwtb3.

21 Kate Julian, "Why Are Young People Having So Little Sex?," *Atlantic*, December 2018, https://tinyurl.com/47zrc2sh.

22 hooks, *All About Love*, 82.

23 Krista Westrick-Payne and Wendy D. Manning, "Marriage, Divorce, and the COVID-19 Pandemic in the U.S.," Bowling Green State University, 2022, https://tinyurl.com/4vh96jt2.

24 Nick Morrison, "Teen Suicides Fell during Lockdown, Rose When In-Person Schooling Resumed, Study Finds," *Forbes*, December 28, 2022, https://tinyurl.com/36eezxas.

25 "Protecting Youth Mental Health: The U.S. Surgeon General's Advisory," 2021, https://tinyurl.com/59nu5usv.

26 Shar Dubey, "How Covid Showed Us the Secrets to Having Better Relationships," *Wall Street Journal*, December 7, 2022, https://tinyurl.com/54b3te9v.

27 "Singles in America," Match, 2022, https://tinyurl.com/2p8a943z.

28 "Singles in America."

29 "Impact of the COVID-19 Pandemic on Marital Quality," Kinsey Institute, March 17, 2023, https://tinyurl.com/y59p6bu5.

30 Farida B. Ahmad, Jodi A. Cisewski, and Robert N. Anderson, "Provisional Mortality Data—United States, 2021," April 22, 2022, https://tinyurl.com/4vunpdbk.

31 "Break My Soul," track 6 on Beyoncé, *Renaissance*, Parkwood Entertainment LLC and Columbia Records, 2022.

32 "Remembering bell hooks and 'All About Love,'" NPR, January 4, 2022, https://tinyurl.com/st2xa6zn.

33 hooks, dedication in *All About Love*.

34 hooks, *All About Love*, 5.

35 hooks, *All About Love*, 6.

36 hooks, *All About Love*, 71.

37 hooks, *All About Love*, 71.

38 Lorena M. Parrish, "Forsaking the Lowly Jesus for Lifestyles of the Rich and Famous, Or How Shall We Be Saved? A Theological Reflection on the Legacy of Christian Attitudes toward Wealth and Poverty, and Its

Impact upon the Black Church" (PhD diss., Union Theological Seminary, fall 2012).

39 S. Craig Sanders, "Why St. Augustine's View of Wealth Is Still Important," Made to Flourish, September 5, 2018, https://tinyurl.com/23zde6te.

40 Kathy Lohr, "Senator Probes Megachurches' Finances," NPR, December 4, 2007, https://tinyurl.com/3n7u73n2.

41 Chris Prentice, "Televangelists, Megachurches Tied to Trump Approved for Millions in Pandemic Aid," Reuters, July 6, 2020, https://tinyurl.com/yum6mspf.

42 Leonardo Blair, "Hillsong Pastors Splurged Tithes on Luxury Life-styles, Former Members Say," Christian Post, January 27, 2021, https://tinyurl.com/5n6p7czn.

43 hooks, *All About Love*, 117.

44 hooks, *All About Love*, 73.

45 Josh Roose, "Trump Still Enjoys Huge Support among Evangelical Voters—and It's Not Only Because of Abortion," The Conversation, October 29, 2020, https://tinyurl.com/5ecme3m6.

46 hooks, *All About Love*, 74.

47 hooks, *All About Love*, 74.

48 Jas 2:26 NKJV.

49 Ira Helderman, "Heeding Erich Fromm's Warning," *Tricycle: The Buddhist Review*, Winter 2020, https://tinyurl.com/ys2rw8hk.

50 John A. Coleman, "Thomas Merton and Dialogue with Buddhism," *America*, July 13, 2012, https://tinyurl.com/3ma4szpa.

51 Peck, *The Road Less Traveled*, 5.

52 hooks, *All About Love*, 79.

53 hooks, *All About Love*, 77.

54 hooks, *All About Love*, 77.

55 hooks, *All About Love*, 79.

56 hooks, *All About Love*, 80.

57 hooks, *All About Love*, 79; 1 Cor 13:1–3 RSV.

58 hooks, *All About Love*, 80.

59 hooks, *All About Love*, 81.

60 hooks, *All About Love*, 83.

61 hooks, *All About Love*, 83.

62 hooks, *All About Love*, 83.

CHAPTER SEVEN

1 hooks, "Hardcore Honey."

2 hooks, "Hardcore Honey."

3 hooks, *All About Love*, 119–20.

4 hooks, *All About Love*, 170.

5 hooks, *All About Love*, 170.

6 hooks, *All About Love*, 171.

7 Lisa Lombardi, "An Expert's Guide to Your Brain in Love," NewYork-Presbyterian, https://tinyurl.com/yck76ux6.

8 A. Pawlowski, "How Long Does Passion Last? Science Says . . . ," Today Show, February 14, 2019, https://tinyurl.com/3jsnzke2.

9 hooks, *All About Love*, 177.

10 hooks, *All About Love*, 139.

11 hooks, *All About Love*, 139.

12 hooks, *All About Love*, 180.

13 hooks, *All About Love*, 181.

14 hooks, *All About Love*, 188.

15 hooks, *All About Love*, 41.

16 hooks, *All About Love*, 39.

17 hooks, *All About Love*, 42–43.

18 hooks, *All About Love*, 42.

19 Eric Adler, "Psychologist's 'Dance' Is Never Solo: To Harriet Lerner, Nothing Is as Important as Connections and Relationships," Knight Ridder News Service, May 1, 1999, https://tinyurl.com/58emtcc7.

20 hooks, *All About Love*, 6.

21 hooks, *All About Love*, 130.

22 hooks, *All About Love*, 164.

23 "State of Nordic Fathers," Nordic Council of Ministers, November 13, 2019, https://tinyurl.com/35rs6krb.

24 hooks, *All About Love*, 210–11.

25 hooks, *All About Love*, 210–11.

26 hooks, *All About Love*, 56.

27 hooks, *All About Love*, 67.

28 hooks, *All About Love*, 134.

29 hooks, *All About Love*, 136.

30 hooks, *All About Love*, 133–34.

AFTERWORD

1 hooks, *All About Love*, 203.

2 hooks, *All About Love*, 202.

3 "Get to Know Our Space," Berea College, https://tinyurl.com/2vpt6fpu.

4 Nadra Nittle, "Changes to AP African American Studies Course Set a 'Scary Precedent,' Advocates Say," The 19th News, February 1, 2023, https://tinyurl.com/45s4x2bn.

5 Mesa-Bains and hooks, *Homegrown*, 30.

6 Mesa-Bains and hooks, *Homegrown*, 30.

7 hooks, *Appalachian Elegy*, 60.

8 George Yancy et al., "A Tribute to bell hooks," *Los Angeles Review of Books*, January 15, 2022, https://tinyurl.com/52ew2hn6.

9 bell hooks, "bell hooks + Jill Soloway—Ending Domination: The Personal Is Political," Eugene Lang College of Liberal Arts at The New School, September 7, 2016, YouTube video, 1:32:37, https://tinyurl.com/bdubz3mt.

10 Mesa-Bains and hooks, *Homegrown*, 59.

11 Mesa-Bains and hooks, *Homegrown*, 23.

12 bell hooks, "Rebel's Dilemma," Lion's Roar, November 1, 1998, https://tinyurl.com/mrx6r7x9.

13 Rebecca Walker, "Op-Ed: bell hooks Was a Mighty Fire," *Los Angeles Times*, December 17, 2021, https://tinyurl.com/jyznyj4p.

14 hooks, *Bone Black*, 3.

15 Walker, "bell hooks."

16 Walker, "bell hooks."

17 Walker, "bell hooks."

18 Walker, "bell hooks."

19 Walker, "bell hooks."

20 Beth Feagan, "bell hooks Lives On," Appalachian Places, April 5, 2022, https://tinyurl.com/3xu3f9sx.

21 Feagan, "bell hooks Lives On."

22 Jennifer P. Brown, "Hopkinsville Memorial Service Highlights bell hooks' Place in the World," Hoptown Chronicle, April 3, 2022, https://tinyurl.com/mrfzks2y.

23 hooks, Yancy, and Brod, "Feminist Future: Mutual Dialogue."

24 Mesa-Bains and hooks, *Homegrown*, 9.

25 bell hooks, *Belonging: A Culture of Place* (New York: Routledge, 2009), 6.

26 hooks, *All About Love*, 202.

27 hooks, *Belonging*, 5.

Index

Adler, Margo, 66, 73
adverse childhood experiences (ACEs), 34
affirmative action, 122
Ain't I a Woman, 1, 35, 63
All About Love, 11, 12, 14, 28, 87–103, 105–19, 121, 122, 127
aloneness, loneliness, 93
altars, 80, 81, 82
American Horror Story, 74
Amos, Emma, 2
Anthony, Susan B., 62
Appalachian Elegy, 67, 122
St. Augustine, 97
Teresa of Ávila, 12, 89

baptism, 42, 43, 52, 123
belonging, 126, 127
Berea College, 12, 121, 125
Bethune, Mary McLeod, 3
Beyoncé, 13–21, 74, 95
Blac Chyna (Angela White), 123
Black Lives Matter, 4, 17
The Bluest Eye, 9, 10, 23, 26, 45, 72, 107
Bone Black, 5, 23–39, 41–54, 110, 114, 124, 126
Black Madonna, 15, 58. *See also* Dark Virgin
Bracciale, Dakota, 76
Bradshaw, John, 116
Branden, Nathaniel, 116

Brown, Brené, 90
Buddhist, Buddhism, 2, 3, 5, 6, 7, 9, 11–13, 15, 16, 17, 18, 19, 21, 22, 46, 49, 56, 59, 67, 68, 79, 82, 84, 87, 99, 100, 102, 113, 119, 125, 126
Burke, Tarana, 70

Cady, Linell, 68
Campus Crusade, 49, 51, 52
Cannon, Katie, 69
capitalistic, capitalism, 5, 6, 11, 13, 14, 15, 20, 21, 29, 38, 41, 62, 72, 73, 87, 95, 98, 99, 112, 119, 121, 130
cathexis, 96
Catholic Church, Catholics, Catholicism, 11, 18, 32, 49, 52, 54, 79, 87, 100, 119
cave, 49, 50, 52, 53
censorship, 112
Charley, Aunt, 36, 37, 41, 44, 46, 47, 49
Charmed, 74
child liberation theology, 28–31, 38, 101
Christians, Christianity, 2, 3, 5, 6, 8, 9, 11, 12, 15, 16, 21, 22, 29, 31, 32, 36, 37, 41, 43, 44, 47–49, 56, 58–60, 63, 66, 67, 68, 69, 71, 72, 77, 78, 80, 81, 83–85, 97, 99, 100, 102, 113, 126, 127

church, 7, 12, 32, 33, 35, 36, 37, 41–46, 48, 49, 50, 52, 53, 54, 55, 56, 57, 61, 69, 72, 77–81, 97, 98, 99, 101, 119
Clinton, Hillary, 4, 75
Cone, James, 25
Coppola, Sofia, 90
corporal punishment, 24, 29, 30, 31, 114, 119
The Craft, 74
Crenshaw, Kimberlé, 21

Daddy Gus, 38, 39, 41, 49, 50, 51, 53, 54, 75, 97
Dalai Lama, 84, 100
Dark Virgin, 15, 58
dead, death, 9, 11, 12, 21, 23, 59, 67, 80, 81, 82, 96, 98, 99, 100, 102, 110, 121, 123, 124, 125, 126, 127
deacon, 37, 38, 41, 43, 53
DJ Lynnée Denise, 21, 93
divine feminine, sacred feminine, 56, 57, 58, 61, 65, 69, 70, 79, 85
Dollar, Creflo, 97
domestic violence, 34, 58, 111
dominance, domination, 6, 9, 16, 17, 18, 22, 25, 29, 37, 43, 57, 59, 72, 73, 74, 83, 91, 99, 111, 112, 113, 115, 116, 126, 142
Douglass, Frederick, 62
Doyle, Arthur Conan (Sir), 59
Drawing Down the Moon: Witches, Druids, Goddess-Worshippers, and Other Pagans in America Today, 66, 73
dreams, dream interpretation, 44, 48, 49, 50, 53, 60, 67, 72, 84, 85, 106, 110, 119, 124
Dyer, Wayne, 72
dysfunctional families, 113, 114, 118, 119, 126

Eminem, 123
enlightened witnesses, 35, 49, 53, 54

Erma, Miss, 33, 34, 35, 36, 37, 38, 41, 53
Eve's Bayou, 73

falling in love, 95, 108, 109
fathers caregiving, male caregivers, 115, 116
Feagan, Beth, 125
feminist, feminism, 1, 2, 3, 6, 8, 9, 10, 12–16, 18, 19, 20, 21, 22, 28, 35, 38, 43, 45, 55–70, 71–77, 80, 85, 88, 90, 91, 105, 111, 113, 115, 116, 121, 123, 124, 125, 127
Feminism Is for Everybody, 28, 43, 55, 56, 58, 59, 65, 66, 67, 69, 71, 72, 74
fire, 25, 45, 49, 50, 69, 124
folk magic, 44, 46, 47, 49, 83
Fox Sisters, 58
Frazier, E. Franklin, 4
friendships, 87, 89, 90, 91, 117, 118, 119
Fromm, Erich, 89, 99, 100, 107
functional families, 116
fundamentalism, 6, 56, 58, 63, 67, 68, 71–85, 98, 123

Gandhi, Mahatma, 100
gender essentialism, 87, 88
Genocchio, Benjamin, 79
The Gift, 73
God, 3, 6, 8, 15, 19, 25, 30, 33, 34, 36, 37, 38, 42, 43, 45, 48, 50, 51, 52, 53, 56, 57, 58, 60, 61, 63, 66, 68, 69, 70, 79, 97, 101, 102
goddess, 15, 56, 58, 60, 63, 66, 79
Grant, Jacquelyn, 68
Grassley, Chuck (Sen.), 97
Great Resignation, 95
Gross, Rita, 68

Hagar, 50
Hạnh, Thích Nhất, 6–8, 12, 16, 21, 99, 100, 125
Harris, Elise, 87–89

Harry Potter, 20, 74
Herrick, Lee, 90
Hillsong Church, 97
Hinduism, 59, 100
homegrown, 15, 58, 77, 80, 82, 122, 122, 126
hoodoo, 47, 48, 71, 77
Hoodoo for Everyone: Modern Approaches to Magic, Conjure, Rootwork, and Liberation, 77
Bell Blair Hooks, 2, 50
House, Silas, 125
humanistic psychology, 18, 87, 99, 119
hypersexualization, 13, 15, 123, 124

imperialist white supremacist capitalist patriarchy, 5, 6, 11, 13, 14, 29, 95, 99, 121
Indigenous peoples, 15, 32, 47, 48, 54, 59. *See also* Native Americans
intersectionality, 21
Isasi-Díaz, Ada María, 69
Islam, 18, 48, 67, 68, 98, 123

Jacob, 89, 109
Jambalaya: The Natural Woman's Book of Personal Charms and Practical Rituals, 64–65
Jay-Z, 17, 21
Jews, Jewish, Judaism, 52, 61, 67, 68, 69, 99
Jesus Christ, the Lord, 7, 8, 30, 31, 33, 35, 37, 42, 44, 48, 50, 51, 52, 68, 78, 79,
Jim Crow, 2, 24, 80
John the Baptist, 52
Julian of Norwich, 57, 58, 85

Kahan, Rachel, 90
Kavanaugh, Brett, 76
Kelly, Anne, 69
Kentucky, 12, 22, 23; Berea, 32, 67, 75, 83, 125, 126, 127

Killing Rage: Ending Racism, 1, 2
Không, Chân (Sister), 12
King, Martin Luther, Jr. (Rev.), 3, 7, 12, 21, 82, 89, 99, 100, 101

Lee, Spike, 19, 21
Lean In: Women, Work, and the Will to Lead, 74–75
Lemonade, 15–21
Lennon, John, 62
Lerner, Harriet, 89, 112–13
Letters to a Young Poet, 53–54
Lewis, C. S., 89
Lil' Kim, 20, 21, 105, 106, 109, 123
Lincoln, Mary Todd, 59
love, self-love, 2, 3, 5, 6, 7, 9, 10, 11, 12, 13, 14, 16, 20, 22, 27, 28–31, 33, 35, 37, 42, 43, 45, 47, 51, 53, 57, 61, 64, 68, 69, 85, 87–103, 105–19

Madonna, 18, 19
magic, magical, 35, 44, 46, 47, 49, 61, 77, 82, 83, 125
Malcolm X, 19, 21, 82, 122
Mandel, Emily St. John, 90
men's rights movement, 111–12
Mernissi, Fatima, 68
Merton, Thomas, 12, 89, 99, 100, 107
#MeToo, 76
Missing Witches: Recovering True Histories of Feminist Magic, 77
Morrison, Toni, 3, 9, 10, 26, 45, 72, 107
Moses, 101, 125
Moynihan, Daniel Patrick, 4
mujerista theology, 30, 56, 69, 85
Murthy, Vivek (US Surgeon General), 94
Muslim, Muslims, 18, 48, 67, 68, 98, 123. *See also* Islam
National Organization for Women, 62
Native Americans, 15, 32, 47, 48, 71, 83, 54, 59. *See also* Indigenous

neopagan, neopaganism, 56, 66, 67, 72–74, 77, 80, 85
New Age, 59, 84, 87, 97, 109
nonviolence, 7, 15, 16
Nour, Fred (Dr.), 108

Odion, Mark (Father), 79
old ways, 43–47, 78, 83, 84
Ono, Yoko, 62
organized religion, 32, 44, 45, 56, 68, 71, 72, 77, 80, 84, 102

pagan, paganism, 56, 59, 60, 65–67, 72, 73, 74, 77, 80, 85
patriarchy, 5, 6, 11, 12, 13, 14, 16, 18, 21, 29, 59, 62, 65, 66, 73–77, 81, 88, 90, 91, 95, 99, 110–12, 114, 115, 121
Peck, M. Scott, 3, 12, 87, 100
priest, 52–54, 65, 66, 71, 100
prosperity gospel, 97, 98

quilts, quiltmaking, 44–46

Ratajkowski, Emily, 90
Reagan, Ronald, 4
Republicans, 4, 97
respectability politics, 18, 20, 21
Revelations of Divine Love, 57
Revolutionary Witchcraft, 77
Rilke, Rainer Maria, 53, 54
ring shout, 48, 78
The Road Less Traveled, 3, 100
Roe v. Wade, 77
Ruether, Rosemary Radford, 68

Saar, Betye, 81, 82
Saiving, Valerie, 68
Salem witches trials, 60, 67
Sandberg, Sheryl, 74, 75
Saru (Sarah Hooks Oldham, Baba), 44–47, 49, 50, 53, 54, 67, 124
The Secret, 97
segregation, 22, 24, 32

Seidler, Victor, 111
self-actualization, 17, 46
sexism, 1, 12, 22, 24, 32, 54, 78, 83, 88, 98, 113, 122
sexual violence, sexual abuse, sexual exploitation, 1, 15, 25, 56, 59, 63, 64, 75, 76
Salzberg, Sharon, 89, 102
single women, single people, 91, 92, 94, 118
single mothers, 3, 5
Sister Ray, 83
Sisters of the Yam, 69, 82–84
slavery/enslavement, 1, 10, 13, 14, 24, 25, 29, 48, 50, 56, 61, 63, 64, 80, 81
The Spiral Dance, 60, 61, 65
spirit, spirits, 49, 50, 59, 124
spiritual practice, spiritual vision, spiritual traditions, spirituality, 2, 6–8, 10–12, 15, 18, 21–22, 32, 38, 42–44, 46–49, 53, 55–70, 71–77, 80–85, 87, 89, 94–103, 109, 113, 116–17, 119, 121, 123, 125, 127
spiritualism, 56, 58, 59, 67, 85
spiritual growth, 3, 84, 87, 89, 102, 103, 107, 113, 117, 119
Starhawk, 60, 61, 65, 69
Steinem, Gloria, 60, 64, 78, 116
Stieg, Philip (Dr.), 108
Stoltenberg, John, 111
suffrage, 56, 58, 59
suicide, suicidal ideation, 26, 28, 32, 52, 94
Supreme Court, 76, 77, 122, 123
Suzuki, D. T., 99, 100
Swedenborg, Emanuel, 58

Tara, 79, 80
Taylor, Linda, 4
Teish, Luisah, 64, 65
terrorist, 14, 15, 19, 89, 111
Time magazine, 13, 14, 15, 18, 19, 20, 76

traditional African religions, West African religion, African-derived religion, 15, 43, 46, 47, 48, 56, 59, 60, 64, 65, 77, 81–84
Trump, Donald, 75, 76, 77, 97, 98, 123
Truth, Sojourner, 59

Vietnam War, 7, 99
violence, 4, 15, 16, 17, 18, 19, 21, 24, 25, 26, 27, 34, 37, 56, 58, 77, 111
vodou, 59, 64, 71
Virgin Mary, Black Madonna, Dark Virgin, 15, 58

Watkins, Gloria Jean, 2, 17, 18, 23–39, 41–54, 55, 126, 127
Watkins, Rosa Bell, 5, 23, 25, 27, 28, 29, 43, 45, 53, 67, 78, 127

Watkins, Veodis, 5, 23, 25, 26, 27, 36, 37, 39, 41, 43, 53, 126
Walker, Alice, 61, 62, 124
Walker, Rebecca, 124
Watson, Emma, 20
Williamson, Marianne, 72, 89
Weems, Renita, 69
welfare, 3–5
Wilson, Jackie, 95
witchcraft, witches, 60, 61, 66, 67, 69, 71, 73, 76, 77, 83, 125
Witches, Sluts, Feminists: Conjuring the Sex Positive, 77
womanist, womanism, 56, 61, 62, 64, 68, 69, 85
women's liberation, 55, 60, 61, 62, 67, 80, 81, 83, 85. *See* feminism

yard shrines, 80, 81, 82
yearning, 45, 68